CAMOUFLAGE & MARKINGS

JAROSŁAW WRÒBEL with JANUSZ LEDWOCH

Luftwaffe 1935-1940

part 1

AJ•PRESS

AIRCRAFT MONOGRAPH 3

P. O. Box 73
80–461 GDAŃSK 45
Tel. (0-58) 23-33-23

English Edition:
BOOKS INTERNATIONAL
69B Lynchford Road
Farnborough, Hampshire GU14 6EJ, England
Telephone: 0252–376564, Fax 0252–370181

Editor in Chief: **Adam Jarski**
Cover painting: **Jarosław Wróbel**
Colour Plates: **Jarosław Wróbel, Arkadiusz Wróbel, Sławomir Zajączkowski**
Book Design: **Jarosław Wróbel, Agencja A.J.-PRESS**
Assistant Editor: **Richard L. Ward**
Translations: **Krzysztof Krzysztofowicz, Wojtek Matusiak**
Drawings: **Arkadiusz Wróbel, Witold Hazuka, Jarosław Wróbel**
English Edition edited by: **Richard L. Ward**
Printed in Poland by: **Drukarnia Oruńska,**
Gdańsk, ul. Małomiejska 41, Tel. (0-58) 39-41-22

ISBN 83–86208–08–2

The Luftwaffe Camouflages; Part 1: 1935–40

In 1939 the Bf 109E–1 fighters of I./JG 20 were in RLM 70/71/65 camouflage. The photograph shows the pre-war-style crosses, their positioning and interesting unit emblem – a white bow – on the cowling.

(R. Michulec coll.)

During World War I, aircraft were already being painted in camouflage colours as it had been found that they were often nearly invisible when seen against the ground, and especially so when painted in the green or brown colours that are predominantly those of the earth.

The development of special camouflage schemes started at this time. As so often happens, such schemes were inspired by nature. The protective colouring used by animals and plants gave an unlimited source of patterns, motifs and decorative designs. A large influence was the German development of segment camouflage, in which a different coloured sequence of polygons was printed on the fabric coverings of their aircraft during the World War I used for covering of German planes during World War I – the so called Lozenge patterns.

The most widely used camouflage consisted of patterns of irregular areas, dots, wavy lines and geometrical patterns.

After the World War I, most European countries abandoned the use of camouflage painting of their military planes, but specially-developed instructions were made available for the rapid repainting of service aircraft in case of military conflict.

During the 1930s, the threat of major war became increased, which induced a rapid expansion of military forces in many countries, including further developments in the art of camouflage painting. The general opinion was that military planes should be painted in the protective colours of the earth – e.g. green, brown, or grey – on the upper surfaces so that they would be hard to see from above or while on the ground, and in sky colours – e.g. mostly blue, grey and black – on the undersides for staying concealed from the enemy while airborn.

The national insignia and code letters were painted on the most visible parts of the wings, fuselage and tail. They were an inseparable element of the colour scheme of a military airplane.

German aircraft on the production line were covered by an electrolytic coating and varnish for climatic protection of the structure; the type of primer and the final colour lacquer depended on the kind of scheme that was used.

During this time the most popular scheme was matt varnish for protection against sun reflections off the aircraft's surfaces, since these reflections could unmask the position of the plane in the air or on the ground. Varnishes were applied by spraying onto precisely described areas and colours. Each painting scheme provided detailed instructions on the correct amount, type and colour of the paint that was to be applied, as well as where it should be placed on the aircraft.

The Luftwaffe used paint schemes in which each colour of the scheme was applied in the shape of a sharp-edged segment. There were a large number of camouflage schemes in existence during the ten years in which the Luftwaffe existed. All military camouflage schemes were regulated by the German Aviation Ministry (Reichsluftfahrtministerium – RLM).

MARKINGS

National insignia are the most important identification element of a military airplane during both peace and war. During the time

Twin-engined Do 23 in RLM 63 light grey camouflage with crosses according to the 1935 standard, black code letters and black swastika in white circle on a red band.

(R. Michulec coll.)

Above: Side view of a Ju 87A–1 with civil code of D – IEAU painted in black on both sides of the fuselage and wings. The vertical tail carries red band with black swastika on a white disc. Note the sharp colour division lines of the RLM 63/62/61/65 camouflage (A scheme) introduced in 1936.

(P. Jarrett via B. Ketley)

The photograph shows well the colour division lines of the RLM 63/62/61 camouflage on upper surfaces of a Junkers Ju 87A of StG 163 "Immelmann" 1938.

(P. Jarrett via B. Ketley)

of the Weimar Republic (1919 – 34), military aviation had been developed clandestinely and German military insignia did not exist. After Adolf Hitler came to power, Germany openly broke with the Versailles Treaty restrictions on its military power. The Luftwaffe was officially created in March 1935. During this time German planes had civilian codes painted on their fuselages and wings. Generally, military aircraft of this era were painted bright silver or grey – green, which acted as a good background for the black code letters and numbers. The new authorities in Germany found these markings insufficient, and on July 6, 1935, they decided to supplement the markings by adding a black swastika (Hakenkreuz) inside a white circle surrounded by a red sash on the left side of the vertical tail. On the right side of the tail was painted a sash in the national colours: black – white – red.

The proportions of this insignia were as follows: the white circle with the swastika was situated in the middle of the length and height of the red sash that stretched from the forward to the trailing edge of the vertical tail. The diameter of the white circle was equal to 3/4 of the height of the sash, and the swastika – with span of 1/2 the height of the sash and a thickness of 1/10 of the sash height – was situated in the centre of the circle. The three-colour sash on the right side of tail (of the same length and height as the sash on the left side) consisted of three

The fourth Junkers Ju 87 prototype – in bare metal with black civil code on the fuselage and wings.

(P. Jarrett via B. Ketley)

Above: Factory—fresh Junkers Ju 87B—1s in 'green' RLM 70/71 camouflage. Well visible brighter shade of the radiator cowling painted RLM 65 blue. Temporary white serials applied on fuselages, repeated in 'normal' size on tails. Summer 1939.
(P. Jarrett via B. Ketley)

A Ju 87B Stuka dive bomber still carries its black civil codes D—IELX on the fuselage (upon arrival in the unit this was overpainted). The splinter pattern of the RLM 63/62/61/65 camouflage is visible. It was introduced in 1936.
(MVT via M. Krzyżan)

horizontal bands of the same height — black, white and red.

An additional marking was introduced in September 1935, based on the World War I German marking — a black and white beam cross (isosceles) — the so-called Balkenkreuz. Its proportion was as follows: the thickness of the arms was 1/4 of their span, and the white border around the outside had a thickness 1/20 of the span.

This kind of cross was painted — according to the tradition — on both sides of the fuselage and on the upper and lower wing surfaces. In the autumn of 1936, the white border of the cross was supplemented by black border with a thickness of 1/30 the span of the cross. The goal was to clearly separate the white border from the background on which it was painted (most planes were painted silver or bright grey-green during this time). With the introduction of the cross as a basic Luftwaffe marking, the tricolour sashes painted on the right side of the tails were gradually removed. They were replaced by the same type of insignia that was painted on the left side of the vertical tail, viz., a red sash with black swastika placed inside a white circle. In September 1938, a decision was made to eliminate the highly visible red sash and white circle that was used as a background for the swastika — leaving only the swastika, with a thin white border having a thickness of 1/6 of the span of the emblem. Shortly thereafter, this white border was supplemented by a thinner black border with a thickness of 1/24 of the swastika's span. However, in spite of this decision, during 1939 there were still large numbers of aircraft which retained the red sashes on their vertical tails. These tails were later painted in a camouflage colour, generally RLM 61 (during this time aircraft were painted in the new type of a camouflage comprising bright grey RLM 63, green RLM 62, russet RLM 61, black-green RLM 70, and dark green RLM 71) — especially after war with Poland began in September 1939.

Special markings were used for the identification of 'enemy' planes during manoeuvres and exercises. The national insignia was covered over by red circles; these were applied using tempera paint 7120, and could later be removed with a rubber jack plane. There are photographs of a Dornier

A Ju 87A–1 W.Nr 5010 of a training unit, as proved by the white 6 on the fuselage. White name "Irene" is painted on the engine cowling. Balkenkreuz according to the 1940 standard.
(P. Jarrett via B. Ketley)

Do 17 E–1 from 7./KG 255 with such markings.

Between late 1939 and early 1940 another modification to the national insignia was introduced – the narrow white borders around the crosse, were widened to 1/8 of the cross span and the thin black border was narrowed to 1/32 of the cross span. This type of cross was painted on the fuselage and lower wing surfaces, whereas the older type of cross (with narrow white borders) was left on the upper wing surfaces because of its lower visibility. Sometimes the situation was exactly the opposite – everything was done to accentrate the presence of the aircraft by painting highly-visible insignia on the upper surfaces. For this purpose huge crosses were painted to cover nearly the entire width of the wing. In KG 26, the He 111 was painted with huge crosses in the old proportion, whereas in KG 53 and KG 27 (which also used He 111s) crosses of the new proportions were used alongside old insignia, but only on the upper surfaces of the wings. The wings of the Do 18 often carried the old kind of crosses supplemented by huge new crosses, but letter consisted only of the white elements – camouflage remaining where the black interior of the cross would have been. Insignia hastily painted in this manner introduced simplifications which were later adopted as standard. Some aircraft of this period had crosses of the new type painted in the standard size on the upper surfaces of the wings (e.g. He 100, Do 215, Hs 126), however, the usual practice was to leave the crosses of 1936-style on the upper surfaces of the wing, with the newer type of cross with widened white borders being painted on the lower surfaces of the wings and on the fuselage sides.

CAMOUFLAGE FOR FIGHTERS

During 1933–35, there were no official instructions regarding the camouflage of fmilitary planes. In 1935, after the official establishment of the Luftwaffe and its rapid development, there was a need to unify ways of painting and lettering service machines. A decision was made that the basic colour would be light green-grey, either RLM 63 Grџngrau or RLM 02 Grau. These two paints probably had the same colour, the different designations originating in the factory names used by paint producers and the official RLM system introduced in 1937/38. Light green-grey (RLM 63) was approximately the same colour that had been used to paint civil airplanes before 1935, and was also used on Luftwaffe fighter aircraft until 1938. It proved to be a good offensive camouflage during the operations of the Condor Legion in Spain (1936–39). In time, the camouflage colour range was enlarged – some Messerschmitt Bf 109s were painted on their upper surfaces in RLM 63 and on their undersides in RLM 65 Hellblau (blue). The demarcations between the colours had sharp edges, which was a general characteristic for most Luftwaffe paint schemes. In the same unit (J 88), the older fighters (e.g. He 51) had a camouflage scheme consisting of three colours – RLM 61/62/63 – on the upper surfaces and RLM 65 on undersides. The camouflage areas were rounded and did not have sharp edges as was the case on the other aircraft in this unit. The Heinkel He 51 C that belonged to Adolf Galland was painted in green and grey colours. In the summer of 1937, the new Messerschmitt Bf 109s began

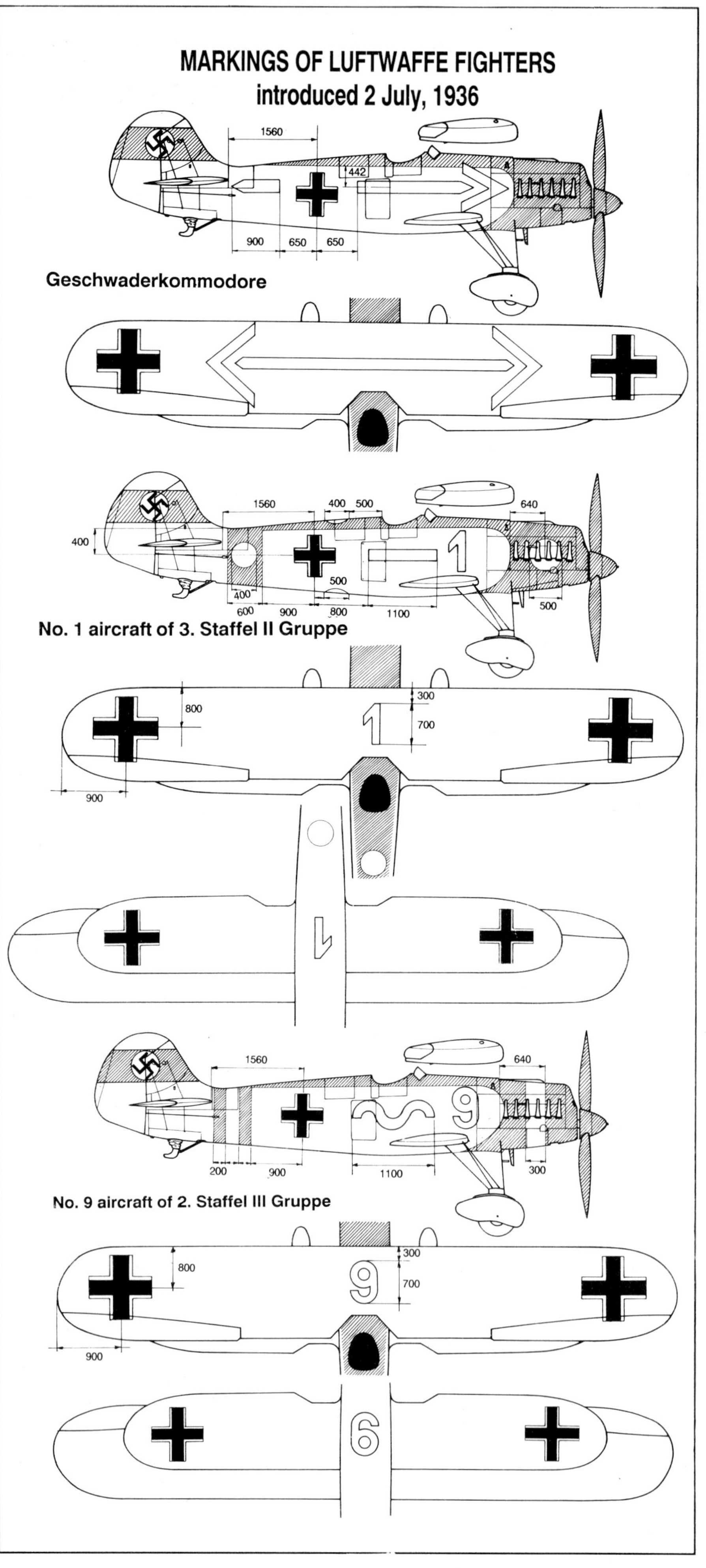

FUNCTIONAL AND TACTICAL MARKINGS OF GERMAN FIGHTERS IN 1933–35 PERIOD

(He 51 for example)

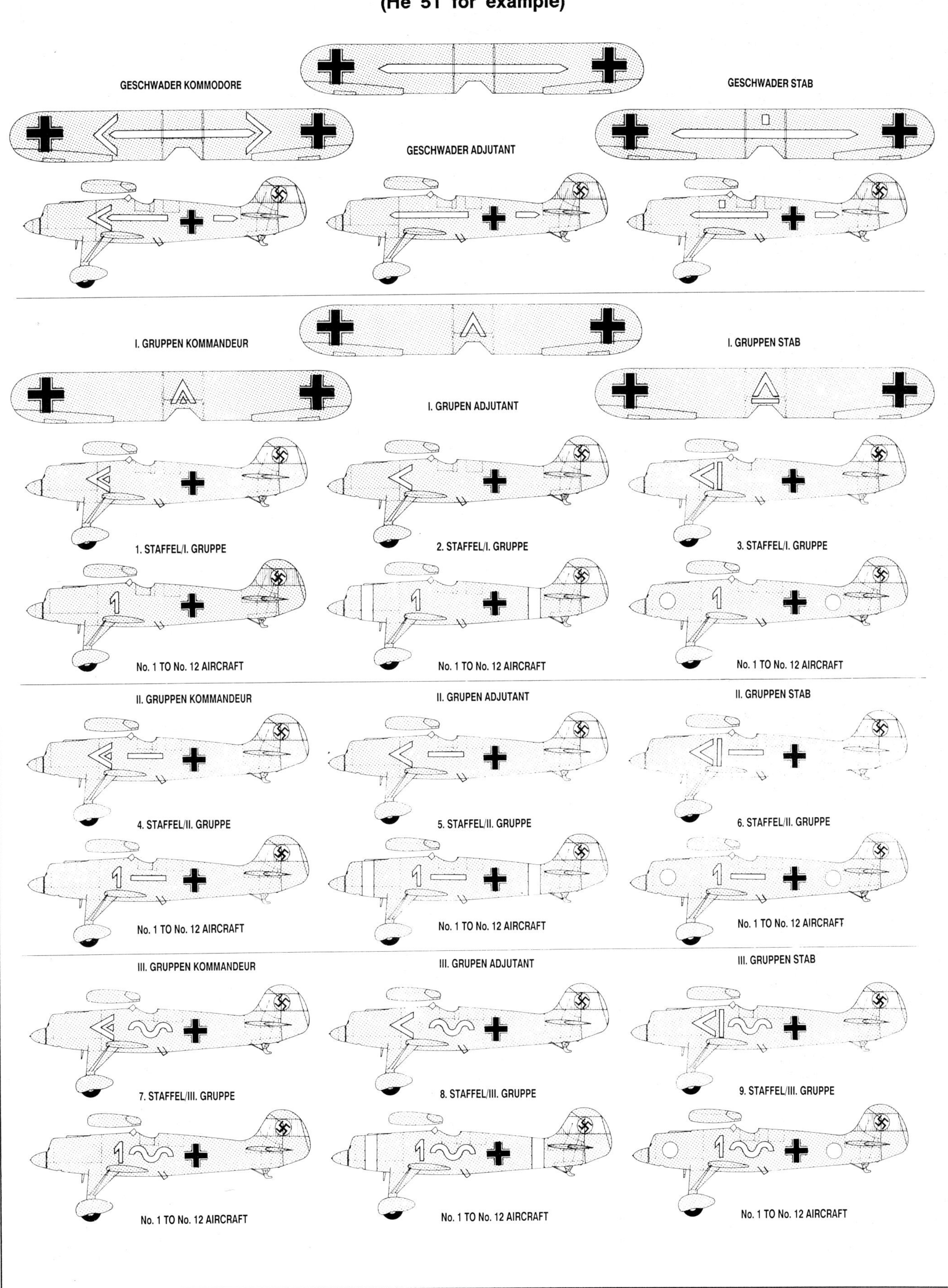

receiving a new scheme developed by the RLM. The upper surfaces were painted in a camouflage that consisted of two tints of green colour: RLM 70 Schwarzgrün (black-green) and RLM 71 Dunkelgrün (dark green), with sharp edges between the colours. The lower surfaces of the airplanes were painted in blue, RLM 65 Hellblau. The Messerschmitt fighter first appear with this camouflage scheme in Spain during September of 1937, e.g. the Bf 109 B–2, 1./J88, 638, to Unteroffizer Ernst Terry. This paint scheme was characteristic of Hitler's air force during the first months of the Second World War, but its life was relatively short. The Luftwaffe offcially abandoned the solid green-grey (RLM 63) camouflage scheme in the autumn of 1938, and in 1939 most German fighters were being painted in the new RLM 70/71/65 scheme. However, some Bf 109Ds (e.g. in ZG 2) were seen that were painted only in the dark green RLM 71 colour on their upper surfaces.

At the end of 1939, modifications in company painting schemes for fighters were introduced – this was during the period of the "Phoney War" ("Sitzkrieg"). Messerschmitt Bf 109s in JG 1 had their fuselage sides and vertical tails painted in a light colour, RLM 02 or RLM 65. This change was caused by the need to use more offensive camouflage schemes, those that made the aircraft less conspievous during air combat: the need for camouflaging aircraft while on the ground was less important, because of German air superiority which made allied attacks on airfields less probable. For example, in II./JG 77 during the winter of 1939/40, some of the Bf 109E fighters had their fuselage sides and vertical tails painted in the blue colour RLM 65, but the upper part of fuselage was left in green camouflage RLM 70/RLM 71.

The division between the lower and upper surface colours was moved upward. At the beginning of 1940, such painting was widely used; at the same time the black-green RLM 70 was replaced by grey-green RLM 02. During the French Campaign in the spring of 1940, in almost all fighter units the camouflage scheme consisted of RLM 71/02 on the upper surfaces of the wings, horizontal tail, and on the upper fuselage, with RLM 65 on the lower surfaces and

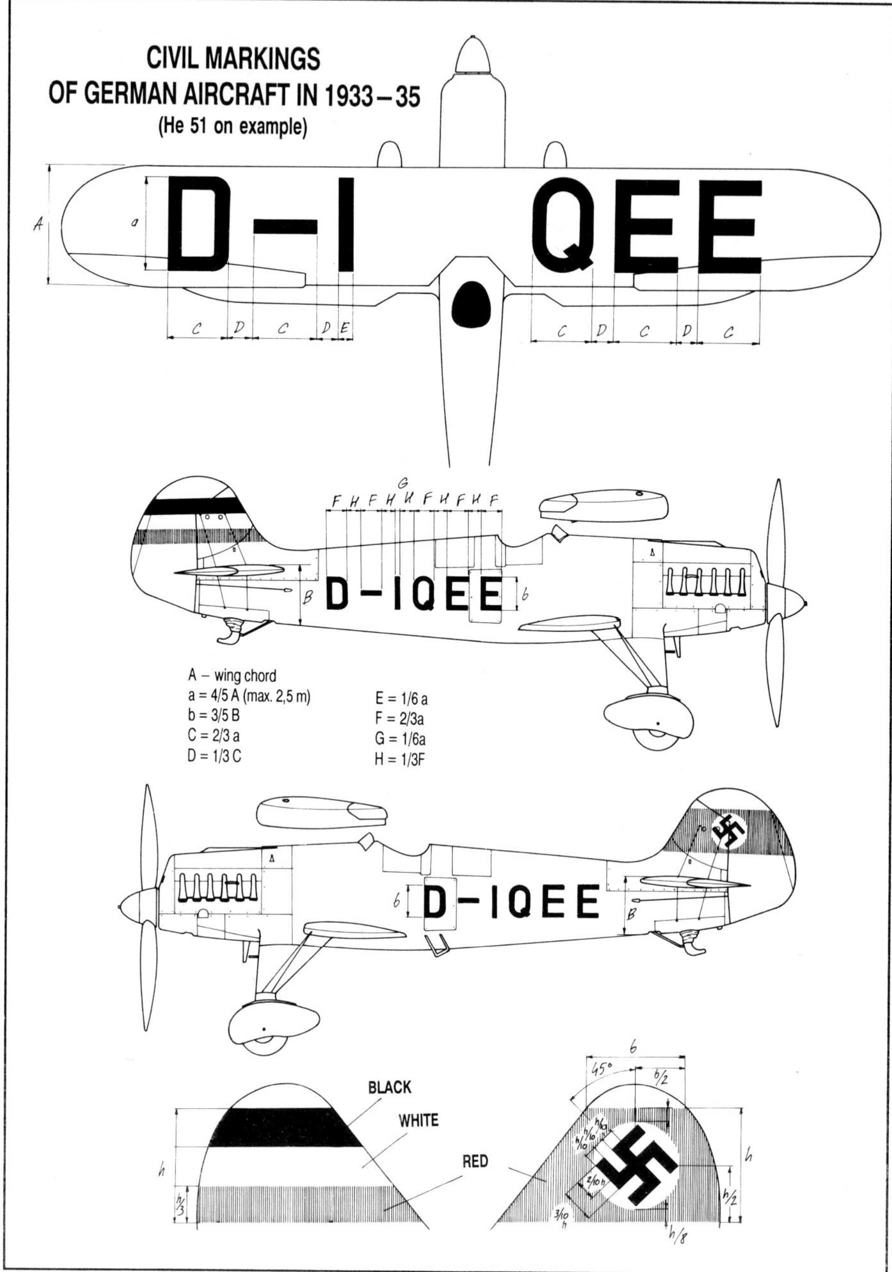

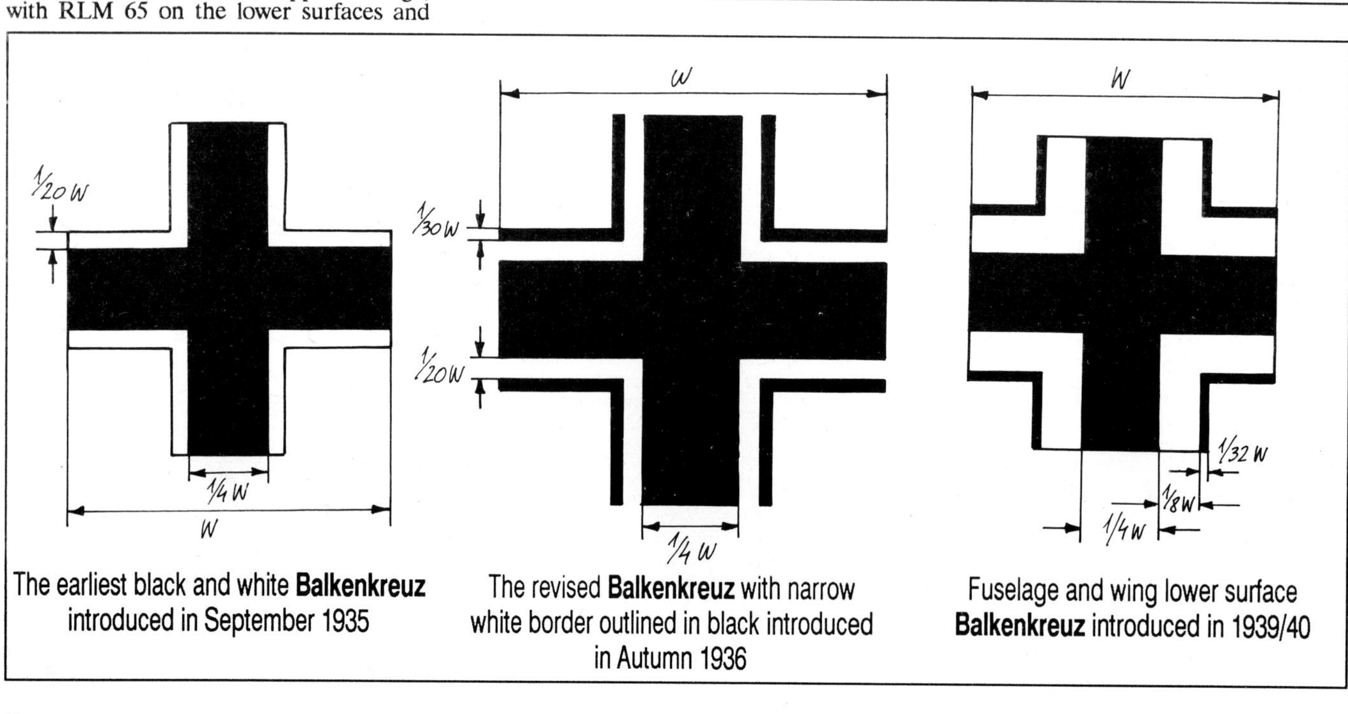

The earliest black and white **Balkenkreuz** introduced in September 1935

The revised **Balkenkreuz** with narrow white border outlined in black introduced in Autumn 1936

Fuselage and wing lower surface **Balkenkreuz** introduced in 1939/40

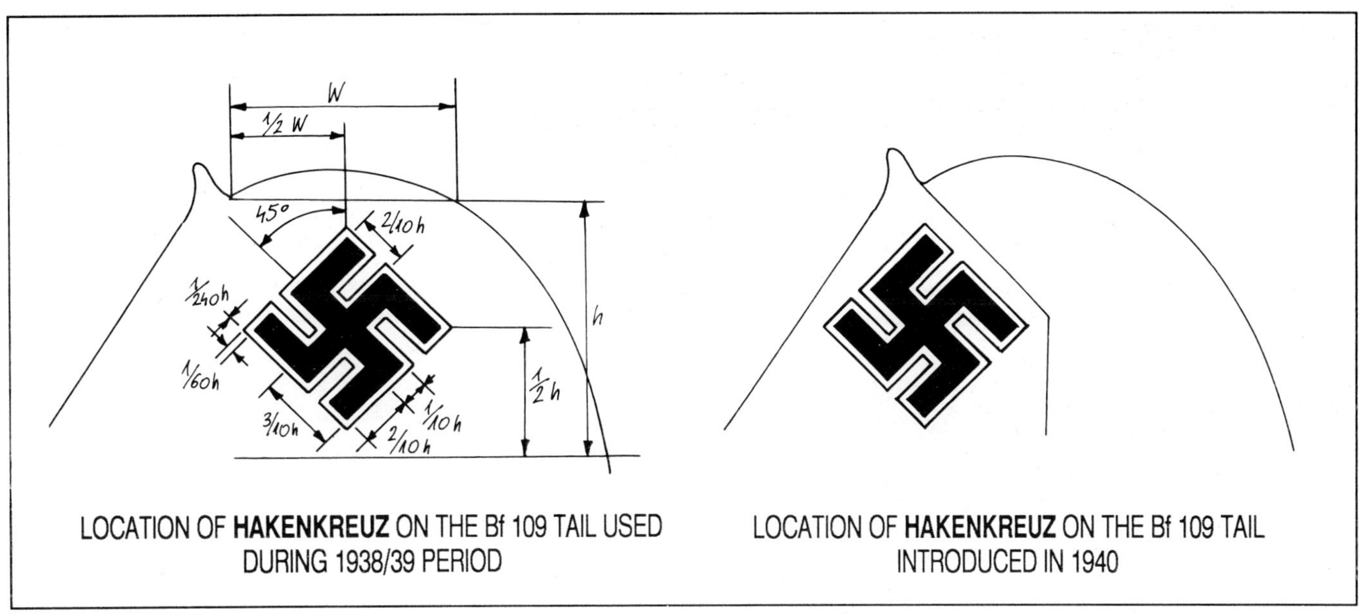

LOCATION OF **HAKENKREUZ** ON THE Bf 109 TAIL USED DURING 1938/39 PERIOD

LOCATION OF **HAKENKREUZ** ON THE Bf 109 TAIL INTRODUCED IN 1940

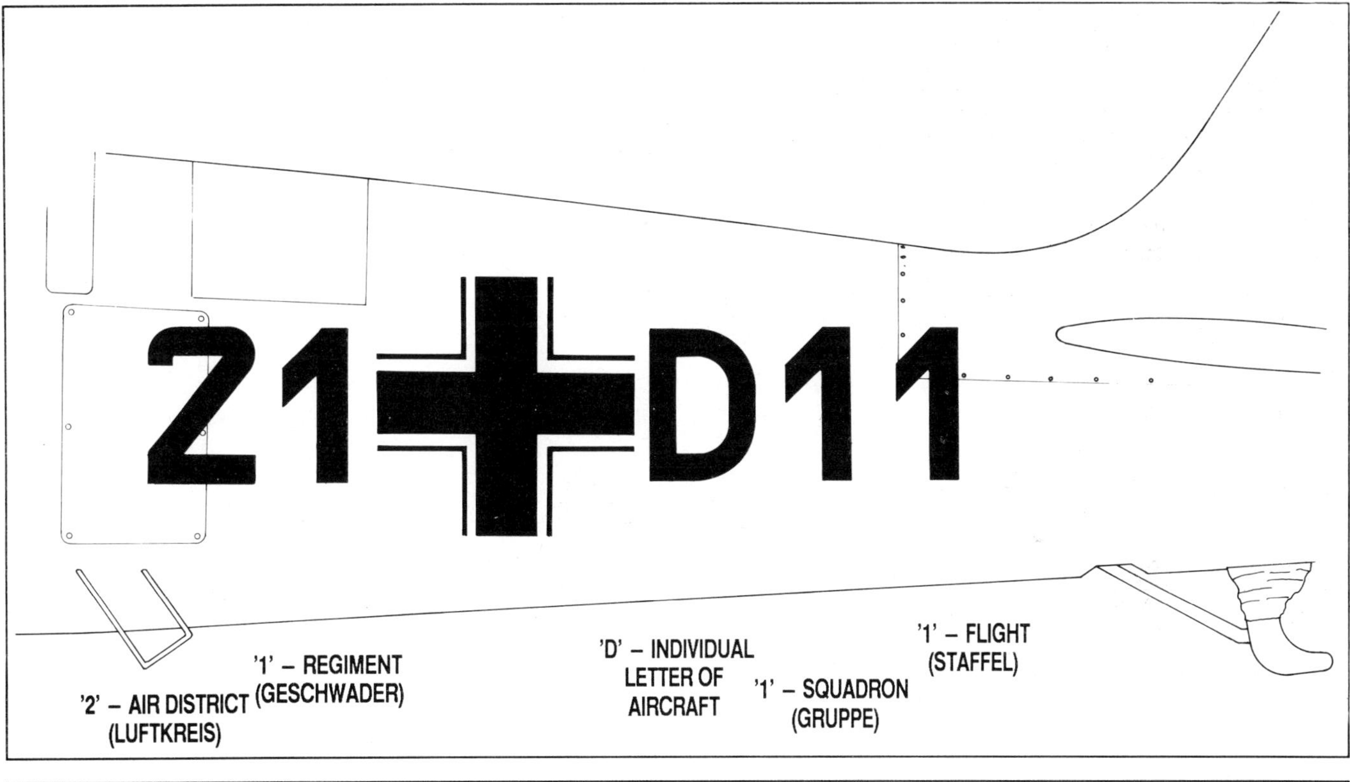

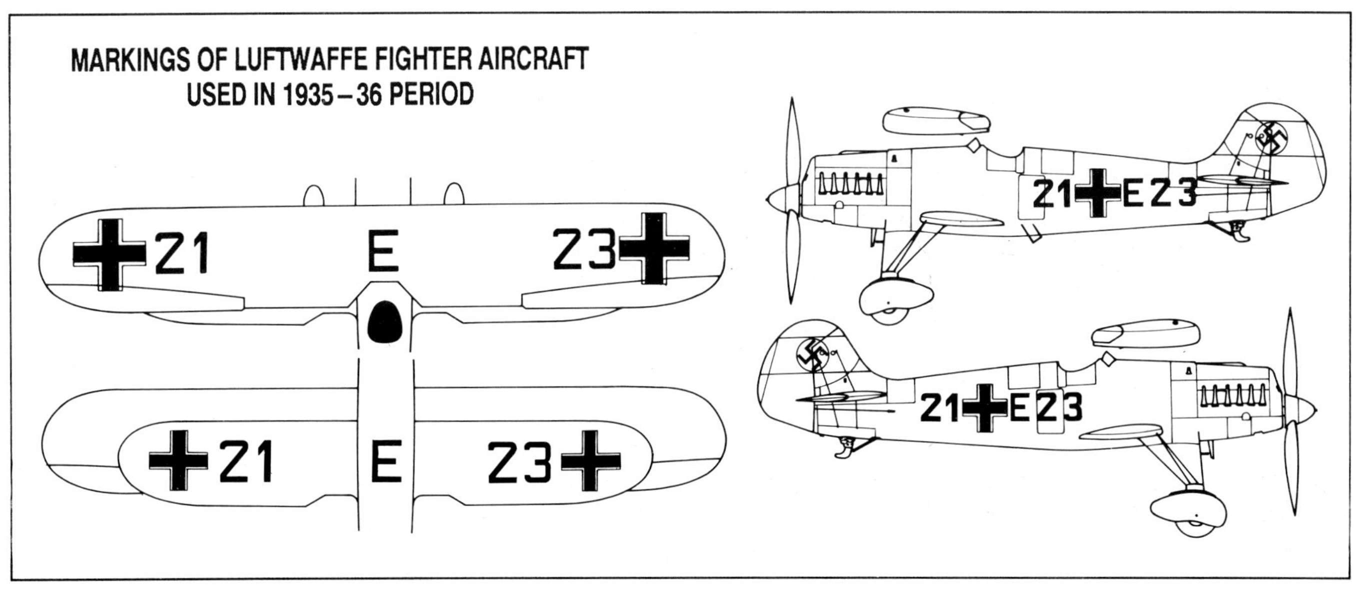

Above: He 51B–2 was also manufactured as a floatplane. Grey (RLM 63) aircraft carries markings as introduced in 1936, 'white 12' in black outline was repeated on upper surface of wing centre section and on the bottom of the fuselage (partly visible). Note that the floats have been partly overpainted with black anti-corrosive primer.

(MVT via M. Krzyżan)

fuselage sides. A number of Messerschmitt fighters were painted in such camouflage as late as the autumn of 1940, but during the summer months of 1940, most of their fuselage sides and vertical tails had been painted in different ways. Often there would be a pattern of small irregular sprayed spots in RLM 02 or RLM 71, but sometimes streaks (e.g. in JG 54) or small dots (e.g. in JG 2) that were painted in by brush. These camouflage supplements were introduced because of the need to better conceal the aircraft that were based at airfields near the English Channel, which were more exposed to allied air attacks. The ideal camouflage would be a selection of colours that would make airplane less visible both in the air and on the ground. Tests with grey colours were made at the

Above: In 1935 the RLM 63 light grey He 51As received civil codes on the fuselage and wings. Black/white/red bands are visible on tail, the other side sported red band with black swastika in white disc.

Below: Three He 51s of JG 132 taxi to runway. They are marked according to 1935/1936 standard – black five-character codes on the fuselage and wings, and have red fuselage noses (JG 132 marking).

(both MVT via M. Krzyżan)

On 15 September 1935 the Balkenkreuz was introduced as the basic Luftwaffe marking. The photograph shows well its proportions. The He 51A–1 fighters are painted in light grey RLM 63 overall. Small individual numbers 1 and 6 on the fuselage and wing centre section are well visible. This type of markings was introduced on fighters in July 1936.

(MVT via M. Krzyżan)

factory and in the field, and what emerged was a range of grey-green camouflages that were the dominant colours painted on Luftwaffe planes used during the Battle of Britain. During the autumn of 1940 Bf 109E–4B, from II.(Schlaht)/LG 2 recieved a new company-developed camouflage that consisted of the new colours RLM 74 Dunkelgrau (dark grey-green), RLM 75 Grauviolett (grey-violet) and RLM 76 Hellgrau (blue-grey) colours. The distribution of camouflage colours were similar to that which had been used before – the upper surfaces of wings, tailplanes and fuselage were painted in the RLM 74 and RLM 75 colours, with the undersides of the fuselage, wings and tailplanes being painted in RLM 76. The sides of the fuselage and the vertical tails were finished with irregular blotches of spots of RLM 70 and RLM 02. The same scheme was probably applied in the autumn of 1940, during the late Battle of Britain period, to the Bf 109 E–4 flown by the famous fighter ace Adolf Galland.

CAMOUFLAGE FOR BOMBERS, RECONNAISSANCE AND TRANSPORT AIRCRAFT

In the first years of the existence of German military aviation in the 1930s, aircraft used by bomber, reconnaissance and transport units were usually painted in silver RLM 01 or light green RLM 63. These paints were applied on all surfaces; on multi-engine aircraft, the engine cowlings and parts of the fuselage and wings were painted in semi-gloss black. This black colour was used in places where oil or exhaust gases were concentrated, staining from which could clearly show up on bright surfaces, although not so much on dark surfaces.

The Junkers Ju 52/3m aircraft flying with KG 152 "Hindenburg" in 1936 had been painted in accordance with this scheme – the basic colour was RLM 63, supplemented by black on the engine cowlings and nacelles, the fuselage nose from engine to cockpit, the main gear fairings and on parts of wing aft of the engine to the trailing edge. White decorative markings were painted on the black main gear fairings. During this time the national markings consisted of the Balkenkreuz on the fuselage and wings and a red sash with swastika inside a white circle on the vertical tail. These were supple-

A reconnaissance He 114 in pre-war scheme typical for floatplanes – fuselage and wings in RLM 02, floats – RLM 01. The aircraft has civil codes.

(P. Jarrett via B. Ketley)

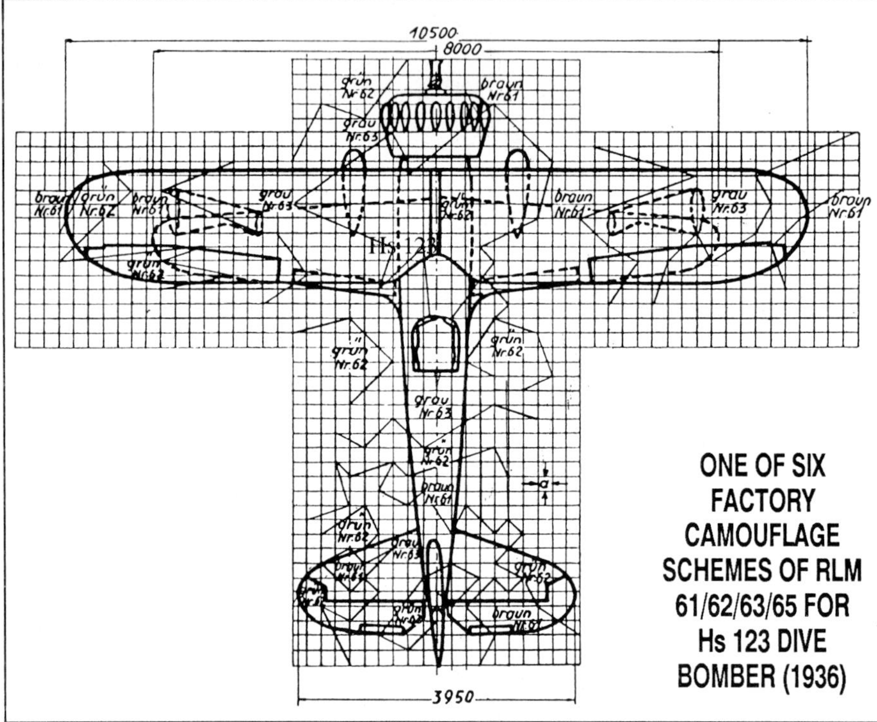

ONE OF SIX FACTORY CAMOUFLAGE SCHEMES OF RLM 61/62/63/65 FOR Hs 123 DIVE BOMBER (1936)

mented by a military code consisting of five letters painted in black; this designated the unit to which the aircraft belonged, as well as its position within the unit.

When the civil war in Spain began in July 1936, the Germans sent the Condor Legion to fight on the side of General Franco's Nationalists. This unit consisted of squadrons with aircraft generally finished in the camouflage of the time, e.g. RLM 63 on all surfaces. During military operations, there was often a necessity to develop more defensive camouflage schemes for bombers. Because airplanes were situated on airfields near the front line they needed better camouflage against an earth background. At the end of 1936 a new camouflage scheme emerged – upper surfaces were painted in three-colour segments with sharp edges – russet (RLM 61 Dunkelbraun), green (RLM 62 Grün) and light grey-green (RLM 63 Grau). Undersides were painted in blue (RLM 65 Hellblau). The use of colours on the upper surfaces was interchangeable – the instructions stated only that sharp edges of different colours should be used, but nothing was said about where a colour should be placed. Areas were filled in generally in the following way: a segment in RLM 63 was situated near an area of RLM 62 that was next to a segment in RLM 61 painted near an area of RLM 63. The pattern was repeated on the uppersurfaces of the entire aircraft.

Another version of this camouflage was used that was the negative of first variant – this gave a large number of variations that could be used when camouflaging aircraft in RLM 61/62/63.

Bombers that operated at night were sometimes painted black on their undersides instead of blue RLM 65. The airscrew spinners were at first painted in just one of camouflage colours, but later they were often painted partly or entirely in bands of squadron colours. During 1936–39, floatplanes and flying boats were usually painted in light green (RLM 02) on all surfaces. However, in some cases the floats of seaplanes and the lower hulls (below the waterline) of flying boats were painted in silver (RLM 01), and the undersides of floats were painted in semi-gloss black anti-corrosion paint.

The primacy of RLM 61/62/63/65 lasted for about two years in the German Luftwaffe. From September 1938 onward, it was ordered that new aircraft should be painted in a new scheme that consisted – as before – of areas with sharp edges, but now the number of applicable colours was limited to two tints of green (RLM 70 Schwarzgrün and RLM 71 Dunkelgrün) on the upper surfaces and blue (RLM 65 Hellblau) on the undersides. The Reichsluftfahrtministerium felt that this scheme was more suitable for the Central and Eastern European theatre.

When World War II started in September 1939, most bomber, reconnaissance and transport aircraft were painted according to this new scheme, and those painted in according to the old scheme could generally be found only in second line or support units. Aircraft produced before 1939 were generally painted in the old camouflage. Gradu-

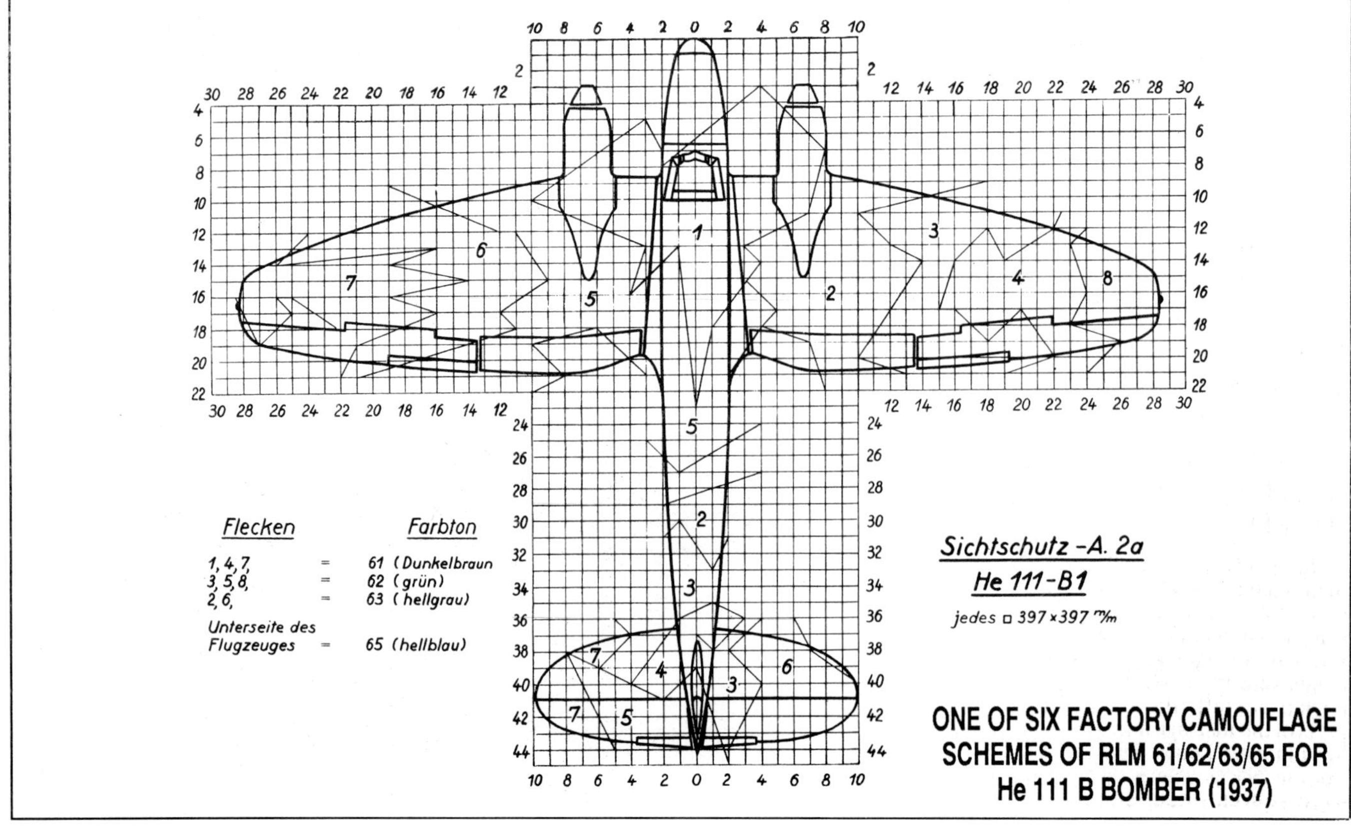

ONE OF SIX FACTORY CAMOUFLAGE SCHEMES OF RLM 61/62/63/65 FOR He 111 B BOMBER (1937)

ally, as the older airplanes went out of service, the pre-war RLM 61/62/63/65 scheme disappeared and was replaced by a new RLM 70/71/65 scheme. However, as late as 1942 on the eastern front in night attack units (Nachtschlachtgruppen), older aircraft (e.g. Hs 123) could still be found with the four-colour camouflage scheme of 1936.

The airscrew spinners were usually painted in RLM 70 as standard. However, in the field, the spinners were often painted in squadron colours (yellow, white, red, green, blue), applied either on the entire spinner, or on its nose, or as a band around it. The propeller was painted in black-green RLM 70. From late autumn 1939, airplanes in marine aviation and coastal units were painted with a scheme in which the upper surfaces were painted in black-green (RLM 72 Grün) and dark green (RLM 73 Grün) segments and the undersides in blue (RLM 65 Hellblau), this including the planing hulls and float undersides of flying boats and floatplanes.

CAMOUFLAGE FOR TRAINERS AND UTILITY AIRCRAFT.

For the basic training of Luftwaffe pilots, gliders were used. These were generally painted in cream-yellow (RLM 05), but they were sometimes also painted in light cream (FAS 1), blue (FAS 2), brown (FAS 3), light green (FAS 4), yellow (FAS 5) and grey (FAS 6). NSFK (Nationalsozialistisches Fliegercorps) gliders had registration numbers painted in black (e.g. D–13650 on a Granau Baby II). From 1 January 1939 onward, the letter 'D' had been replaced by the letters 'WL', but only on some gliders, in spite of the decision, large numbers of them flew with their old registration numbers. Many of them still had their vertical tails painted with the red sash and swastika in a white circle even if they had been withdrawn from service units a long time before.

Until 1939, training aircraft belonging to the Luftwaffe were painted entirely in silver (RLM 01). Gradually, silver was replaced by a more camouflaging light grey-green (RLM 02). These aircraft were painted with standard insignia – crosses and swastikas – and supplementary registration numbers were painted on the wings and fuselage. As in the case of gliders, the registration number started with the letter 'D' before 1 January 1939 and later with the letters 'WL'.

In 1939 the new camouflage used elsewhere in the Luftwaffe (RLM 70 & 71 for

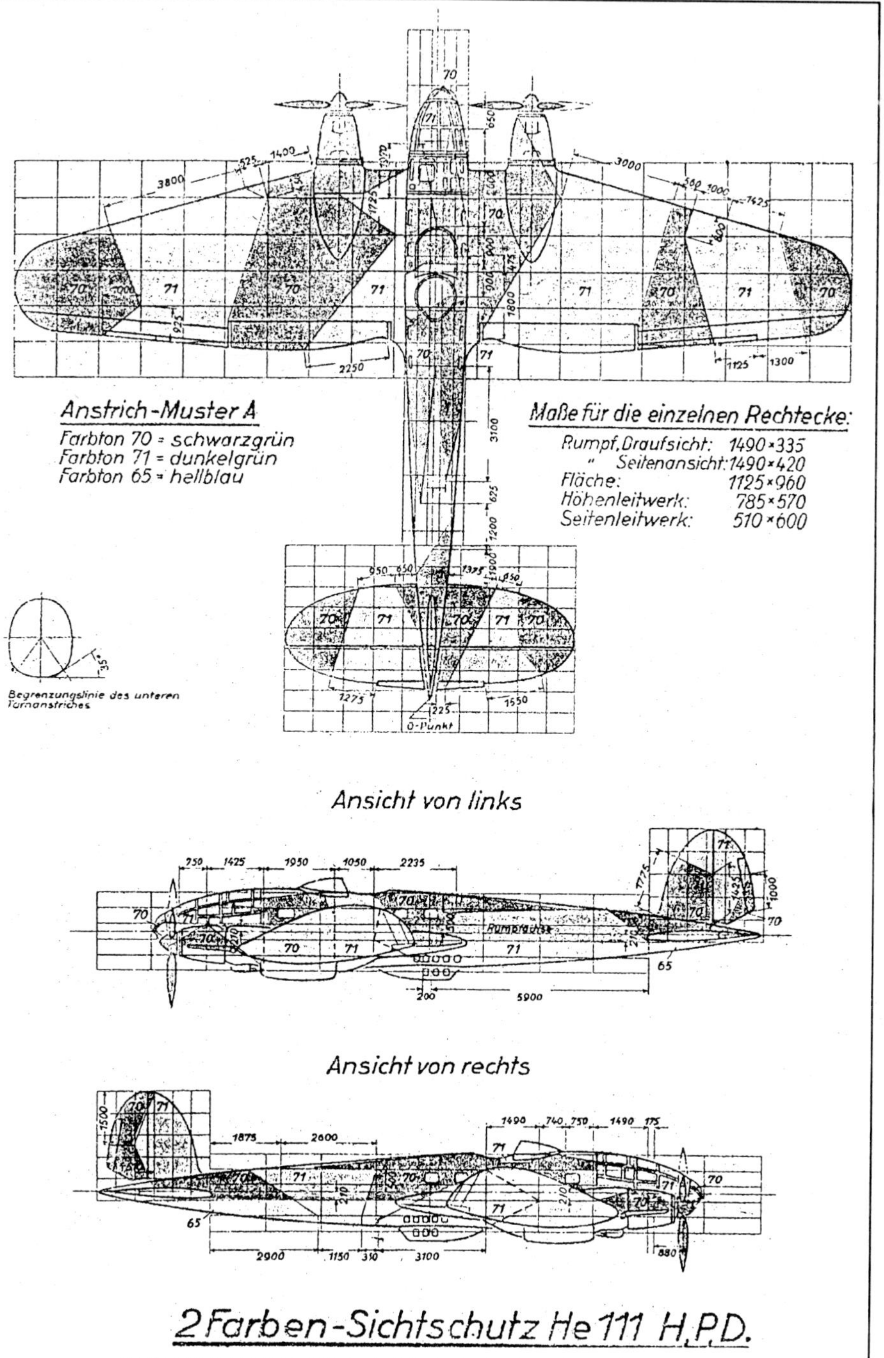

Anstrich-Muster A
Farbton 70 = schwarzgrün
Farbton 71 = dunkelgrün
Farbton 65 = hellblau

Maße für die einzelnen Rechtecke:
Rumpf, Draufsicht: 1490×335
" Seitenansicht: 1490×420
Fläche: 1125×960
Höhenleitwerk: 785×570
Seitenleitwerk: 510×600

Begrenzungslinie des unteren Tarnanstriches

Ansicht von links

Ansicht von rechts

2 Farben-Sichtschutz He 111 H, P, D.

FACTORY CAMOUFLAGE SCHEME OF RLM 70/71/65 FOR He 111 H AND P BOMBER

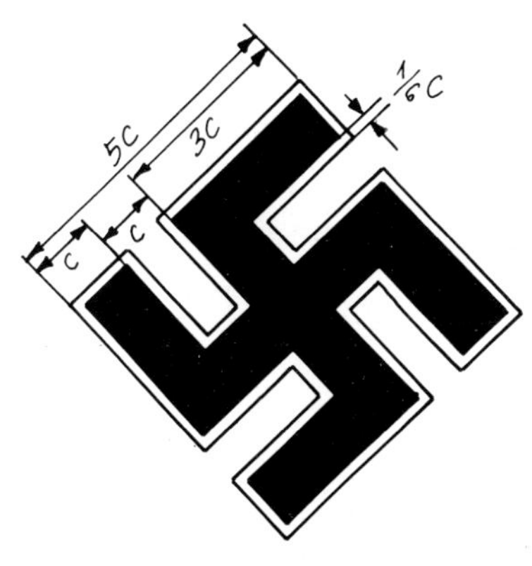

REVISED HAKENKREUZ

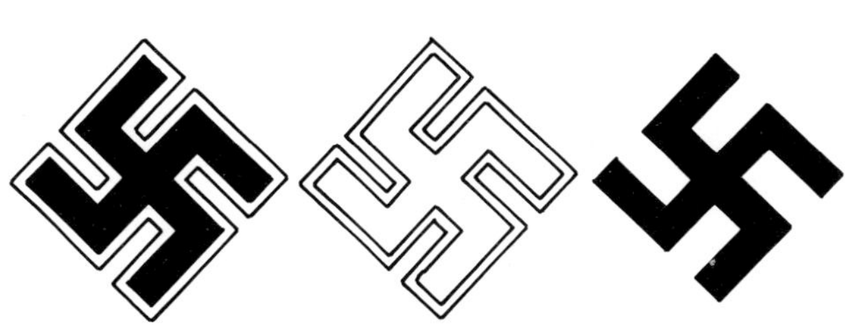

THE SWASTIKAS USED DURING 1938–40 PERIOD

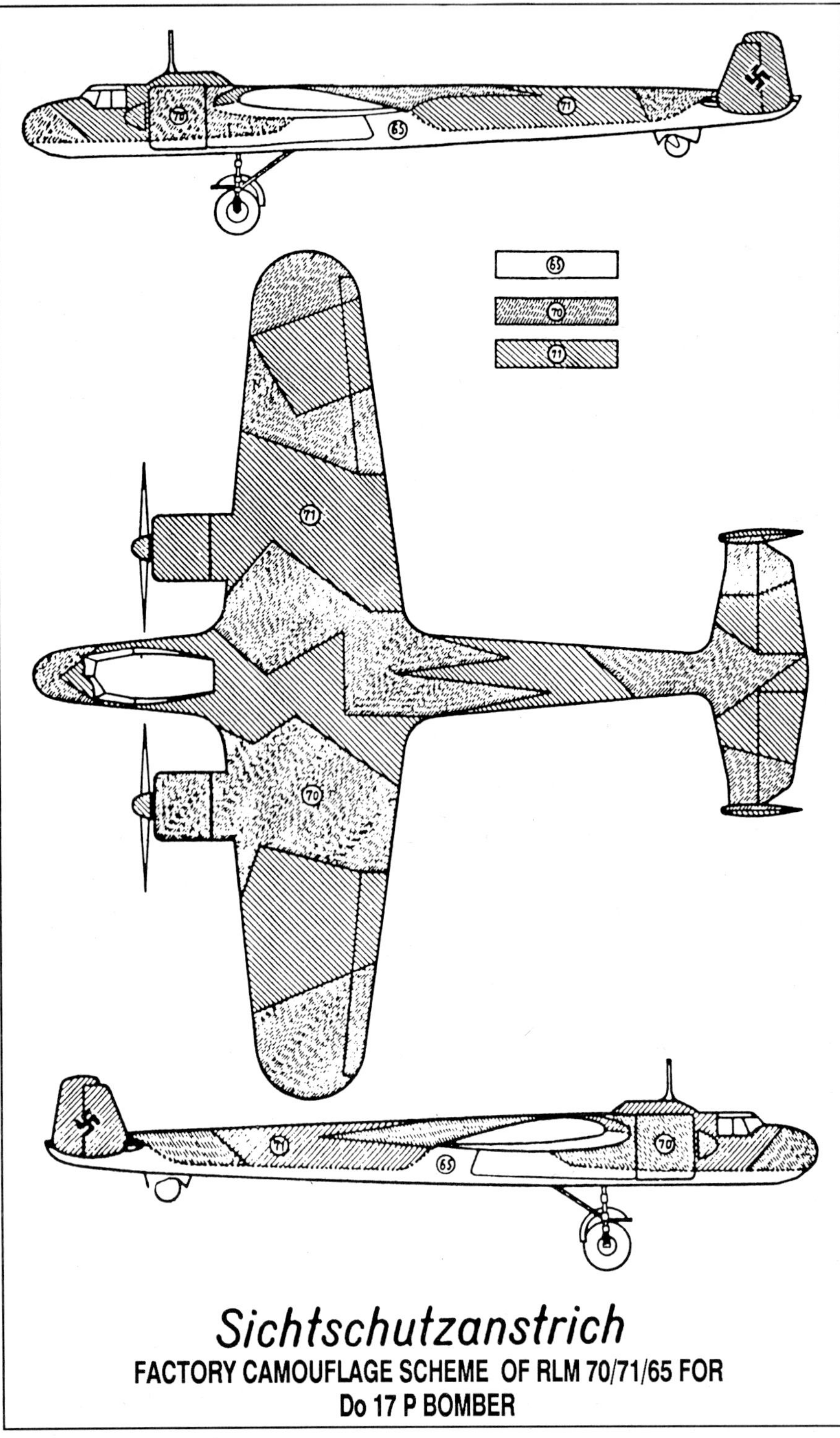

Sichtschutzanstrich

FACTORY CAMOUFLAGE SCHEME OF RLM 70/71/65 FOR Do 17 P BOMBER

uppersurfaces and RLM 65 for undersides) was introduced for trainers and utility types.

Sometimes supplemental markings were used for easier identification of training aircraft in the form of, for example, white or yellow bands painted on the fuselage (in blind – piloting schools). Camouflage of utility and staff transport airplanes (e.g. Bf 108, Junkers W 34, Fi 156 "Storch", Fw 58) was generally the same as for training types; during 1935 – 38 the entire aircraft was painted in cream-yellow (RLM 05), with light grey-green (RLM 62 or RLM 63) later being used. From 1938, the standard RLM 70/71/65 scheme was introduced. In addition to the standard Luftwaffe identification markings (Balkenkreuz, Hakenkreuz), codes were introduced onto the fuselage and wings which identified the unit to which the aircraft belonged.

INTERNAL PAINTING

Before and during first part of the war, the colours of internal surfaces were differently painted depending on the material and the part of the aircraft. Directive L. Div 521 of November 1941 precisely stated that the inside surfaces of the cockpit and other parts of fuselage that were covered with glass should be painted in grey-black (RLM 66) as anti-reflection cover. Other internal surfaces were to be painted generally grey-green (RLM 02). Inside the cockpit, many parts were painted in tints of grey, e.g., the instrument panel was painted in grey (RLM 41), while levers, handwheels, and different kinds of buttons were painted in bright colours for easier identification. These colours were typically red (RLM 23) and yellow (RLM 04). The internal surfaces of wings and tails were electroplated during production to give a high quality anti-corrosion cover, and provided a metallic gold tint similar to that observed in food cans. Parts made of wood were painted with special light yellow-green (RLM 99) protective paint.

Before 1937, the inside surfaces of engine cowlings were left with their original electroplated colour, but later they were painted in grey-green (RLM 02). The protective fire wall between the engine and the cockpit was generally not painted on the engine side, but was painted in grey-green (RLM 02) on the cockpit side.

Internal tanks were painted as follows: fuel — yellow; oil — brown; cooling fluid — green; fuel installation — blue, fire installation — red. Engine serial numbers were painted in white or yellow on the engine block.

MARKING FOR FIGHTERS

Military aircraft markings were a supplement to the national insignia and helped in rapid identification, which unit the aircraft belonged. The code letter for German civil aircraft was D — Deutschland. Previously, letter — number symbols such as D – 1267 were used. For example, an Arado SSD — D – 817, or a Koolhoven FK 33 airliner D – 1250.

Beginning in 1933 a four-letter code was

A group of Messerschmitt Bf 110Bs of I./ZG 76, 1939. RLM 70/71/65 camouflage of 1938, Balkenkreuz of 1936-shape (narrow white arms), codes 2N + KK black, except the individual letters K, H, I and F, which were red with white outline (in the Staffel colour).

(P. Jarrett via B. Ketley)

Above: A light grey RLM 63 Junkers Ju 52/3mg3e of Flugzeugführerschule (C) at Lechfeld in the 1938-style markings — black military codes S7+L15 on the fuselage and wings, Balkenkreuz with narrow white outlines, black swastika in a white disc on a red band. Note the black glossy areas on the fuselage and engine nacelles, typical for the Junkers.

(MVT via M. Krzyżan)

introduced, e.g. D–ASFF. The old system was used in parallel until mid–1936. In the new system, it was possible to use the first letter after the D– in the registration to define the aircraft category, i.e. empty weight, number of passengers and number of engines. The code is given in the table on page 19.

The last three letters in the registration number were in the AAA–ZZZ range. The following registration numbers were possible: DYAAA–DYZZZ, DEAAA–DEZZZ, DIAAA–DIZZZ, DOAAA–DOZZZ, DUAAA–DUZZZ, DAAAA–DZZZZ.

Group of codes DIAAA–DIAAA were reserved for military aircraft prototypes. The first fighter Reklamefliegerabtailung Arado Ar 65 had a marking that started from D–IAAA (the first plane in the series). The Do 15 flying boat had a category C code e.g. D–ABAS, and a He 111 C–02 "Leipzig" category C code also: D– AQYF. Training types generally had codes of the A2 category e.g. Klemm KL 25d: D–EPAK.

Interestingly enough, some of the markings of aircraft built for training purposes (Fokker D.VII fighter from the Huffer Factory in Munich) had codes reserved for military aircraft e.g D–IHOT. Famous from the World War I period, the "Flying Razor" was, in 1938, still considered formidable military aircraft!

The registration number was always painted in gloss black on the wings and fuselage. Technical data about the plane was painted on the starboard rear fuselage; this consisted of information about the owner's name and address, empty weight, useful weight, maximum take-off weight, maximum number of crew, aircraft category and the date of last general inspection. Letters in the data had a height of 25 mm and a width of 4 mm, and were applied using a stencil, mostly in black or red.

Above: Scramble — the pilot hurries to his Bf 109E–1 'red 7' of 2./JG 20 (8./JG 51 from June 1940). The RLM 70/71/65 camouflage, 1936-style crosses (narrow white arms), the engine cowling has an interesting unit emblem — black cat on a white circle.

(MVT via M. Krzyżan)

Below: Interesting emblem applied on cowling of a Messerschmitt Bf 109E–1 painted in 'green' RLM 70/71/65 camouflage (1939).

(P. Jarrett via B. Ketley)

Factory fresh Bf 109B–1s painted according to the new (1937) pattern. 'Green' splinter fields of RLM 70/71 on upper surfaces (note the division lines between contrasting colours), while undersurfaces in RLM 65 blue. The tails sport red bands with black swastikas on white discs.

(P. Jarrett via B. Ketley)

The following is a sample of information that was painted on a He 46:
FLUGZEUGHALTER: TECHNISCHE SCHULE (owner)
BERLIN ADLERSHOF (address)
GRUPPE: LB1 H4 (class)
LEERGEWICHT: 1725 KG (empty weight)
GESAMTLAST: 545 KG (useful weight)
HOCHSTZUL.: 2270 KG (maximum take-off weight)
PERSONENZAHL: 2 (crew)
LEITZE PRAFG: 18.11.37 (last general inspection)

At the end of 1935, the civil code was replaced by a five-symbol military code e.g., 21+E23, in which the first number denoted the Air District (Luftkreis), and the second number the Group (Geschwader) in the Air District. At this time, there were six Air Districts: I in Königsberg, II in Berlin, III in Dresden, IV in Münster, V in München and VI in Kiel. The third space was reserved code letter of the aircraft in the squadron; the fourth character was a number that indicated the wing (Gruppe), and the fifth designated the squadron (Staffel). The code number was painted on both sides of the fuselage (the first two symbols before cross, the rest after) and on the wings centred between the crosses so that one code letter was placed on the axis of aircraft. Some Fighter Groups (Jagdgeschwadern) were given honourable titles in this period; among them was JG 132, which was named "Richthofen" in memory of the most famous World War I fighter pilot, the "Red Baron", Manfred von Richthofen. At the same time, the aircraft of JG 132 had their noses painted red (and later also their rear fuselages and bands on the fuselage).

The same situation existed for JG 134 – that unit was named after SA member Horst Wessel, who was killed in a street brawl. The noses of aircraft in this Group were painted in russet – the same colour as the shirts of SA members.

The same rule was used in other Groups, and began a system of supplemental Group markings:
JG 131 (Jessau) – black,
JG 132 (Doberitz) – red,
JG 134 (Dortmund) – russet,
JG 232 (Barnburg) – green,
JG 233 (Bad Aibling) – blue,
JG 234 (Cologne) – orange.

In the autumn of 1940 Bf 110 Cs of II/ZG 76 still carried the pre–war 'green' camouflage of RLM 70/71/65. The photo shows clearly the arrangement of Balkenkreuzes and codes (M8+CP), the individual letter (here C) was painted in the Staffel colour on both fuselage side and wings. Note the additional red-and-white sharkmouth, painted on Bf 110s of the Gruppe, as well as the personal emblem under the cockpit – a red heart (with two flags beside: the Belgian and the French), and three white bars on the fin to mark air victories.

(MVT via M. Krzyżan)

Above: Bf 110 in factory fresh painting — the pattern of Dunkelgrün RLM 71 and Schwarzgrün RLM 70 areas is well visible. Crosses on the fuselage and wings have narrow white arms and the swastika applied on both fins and rudders mean this photo shows an aircraft of 1939 vintage.

(P. Jarrett via B. Ketley)

Above: In the foreground a row of Arado 68s in light grey camouflage with black fuselage tops and black crosses, introduced in 1935. In the background are the Heinkel 45s still with civil codes on the fuselage.

(R. Michulec coll.)

In spite of orders to introduce this system of markings, a new method of designation had slowly been applying in Groups; even in the middle of 1936 Ar 68 planes from JG 143 were dovoid brown bands on the engine cowling. Sometimes aircraft had both markings systems; He 51 from I./JG 132 had a code (e.g. 21+D11) and the engine cowling painted in red. In II./JG 132, He 51 planes had a names painted in white on the engine cowlings, e.g. "Panther", "Jaguar", "Leopard", "Tiger" and others.

In 1936 each Fighter Group (Jagdgeschwader) comprised 117 aircraft divided into three wings of 36 machines each. Each wing consisted of three squadrons of 12 aircraft. The squadron was treated as a basis of the structure and from this point of view a decision was made to simplify the markings system. Instruction LA Nr. 1290/36 (valid from 1 September) issued 2 July 1936 introduced the new system of markings in which each aircraft in the sqadron was attributed a number between 1 snd 12, painted in white with a black border on the front of the fuselage and on the upper and underside of the centre section of the wing. Size of the numbers was the same in all positions. Affiliation to the squadron was marked by the absence of any symbol (squadrons 1, 4, 7) or by white bands around the front and rear of the fuselage, on the fuselage back and underside (squadrons 2, 5, 8); or by white circles on the front and rear of the fuselage, on the fuselage back and underside (squadrons 3, 6, 9). Because of the bright grey camouflage of fighters in this period, white markings could be of low visibility, and were given wide bands in group colours as backgrounds. Squadron commanders aircraft did not have special markings, but it became the custom to give them the number '1'. Aircraft belonging to the Gruppe could be recognised by white symbol with black border painted just be-

Below: A group of naval pilots of Flugzeugführerschule (See) in Stettin. In the background He 60 floatplanes can be seen in RLM 63 grey-green painting. The floats were painted silver (RLM 01). On the fuselage are black military codes, introduced in 1936.

(R. Michulec coll.)

Factory painting scheme on Bf 109E–4/B W.Nr. 1361 – top: RLM 02 grey and RLM 71 green, bottom: RLM 65 blue. Balkenkreuz in the 1940 standard (wide white elements). When in service the black factory callsign on the fuselage would be replaced by the aircraft number in Staffel and Gruppe marking.

(MVT via M. Krzyżan)

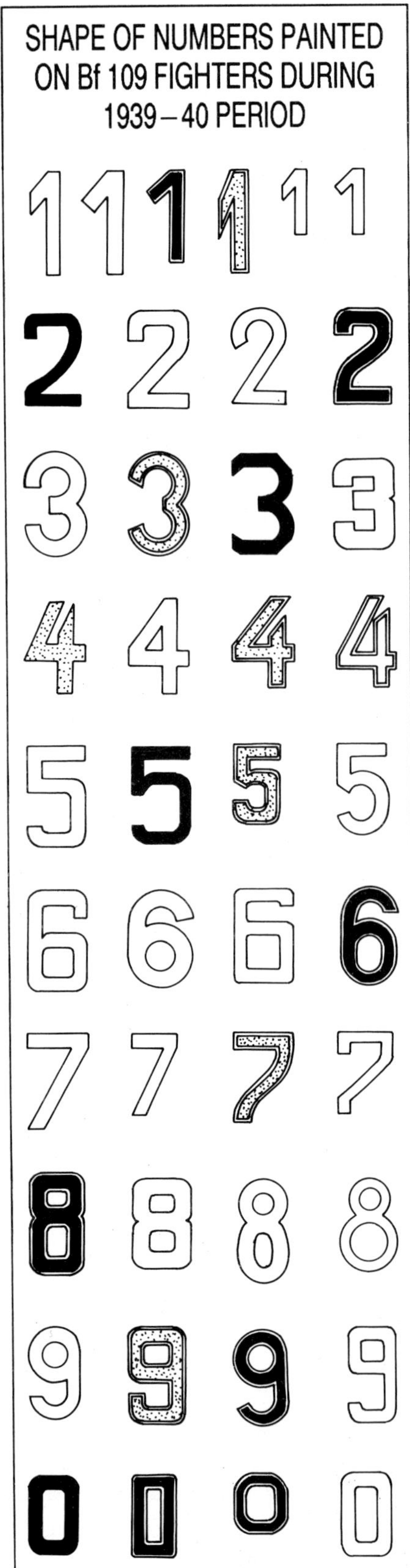

Above: Bf 109E–4 'yellow 3' after an unfortunate landing. Scheme and markings are typical for the Battle of Britain period, fuselage top and wing upper surface covered with segments of RLM 02/71, fuselage sides and lower surfaces in RLM 65. Quick identification markings are yellow nose and wingtips.

(P. Jarrett via B. Ketley)

Below: The upper surface of starboard wing of the Bf 109E–3 shows the colour pattern of grey (RLM 02) and green (RLM 71), fuselage side is RLM 65 blue – a standard in Luftwaffe during early months of 1940.

(M. Murawski via A. Jarski)

Above: A Do 17 E–1, 54+F37 of KG 255 pictured over Germany during an exercise in September 1938. Typical four-colour camouflage of RLM 61/62/63/65 introduced in 1936. is well visible During these exercise the national insignia were overpainted with red discs. *(J. Wróbel coll.)*

Aircraft's registration system of the various specific categories

Class	Registration	Personnel and Weight	Remarks
LANDPLANES			
A1	D–Y...	1 person, all-up weight 500 Kg	
A2	D–E...	1 to 3 persons, all-up weight 1,000 Kg	
B1	D–I...	1 to 4 persons, all-up weight between 1,000 and 2,500 Kg	(Note: This registration group was originally listed as D–J... but was apparently never used, this class are registered in the D–I... rangel)
B2	D–O...	1 to 8 persons, all-up weight between 2,500 and 5,000 Kg	
C	D–U...	Single-engined, all-up weight in excess of 5,000 Kg	
	D–A...	Multi-engined, all-up weight in excess of 5,000 Kg	
SEAPLANES			
A1	D–Y...	1 person, all-up weight 600 Kg	
A2	D–E...	1 to 3 persons, all-up weight 2,200 Kg	
B	D–I...	1 to 4 persons, all-up weight 5,000 Kg	
C	D–A...	Multi-engined, all-up weight in excess of 5,000 Kg	

hind the number on the fuselage; I Gruppe had no symbol, II Gruppe had a horizontal bar, and III Gruppe a wavy line. Wing commanders had been flying aircraft without numbers, but instead were painted double chevrons (white with black borders). Groups (Geschwadern) were identified by the colour of the nose, fuselage decking, and bands on the fuselage sides. Group commander's aircraft had only white chevrons and long bars with red borders. The last important change in Luftwaffe aircraft marking was introduced in 1938 when each squadron was assigned a different colour in which the numbers and identification emblems on the fuselage were painted. Squadrons 4, 7 and 10 had the emblems in white with black borders, squadrons 2, 5, 8 and 11 in red (very rarely black), squadrons 3, 6, 9 and 12 in yellow (very rarely in brown) with black or, again only rarely, white borders. The number was usually painted ahead of and near the fuselage cross side, and the wing symbol in the squadron colour was situated aft of the cross. The 1st Wing had no identify emblems, the 2nd Wing had a horizontal bar, the 3rd Wing previously had a wavy line but from 1941, a vertical bar, and the 4th Wing had a black circle with white outlines or a small cross, similar to a Balkenkreuz.

Group status was defined by emblems painted on the fuselage sides, generally near the cockpit or on the engine cowling.

Emblem of I./ZG 2 below windscreen of a Messerschmitt Bf 109D – an archer in a silver circle. Stencilling is well visible. Camouflage is RLM 71 (top) and RLM 65 (bottom).
(P. Jarrett via B. Ketley)

A Dornier 18 on a take-off catapult. The aircraft operating over sea received camouflage of RLM 73/72 greens with blue-grey hue. On the engine cowling was shown individual letter 'C'. Under wing surfaces feature increased size Balkenkreuz, painted in 1940.

(R. Michulec coll.)

Emblems were in form of colourful drawings often of heraldic character in which appeared stylised animals, plants, side-arms, or designs which belonged to fighter aviation elements. Rank insignia for commanders, aides-de-camp, engineers and staff officers were painted in white or black with white borders in the form of chevrons and bars on the fuselage, often of considerable size. Single engined fighters used by night fighter units (Nachtjagdgeschwadern) were a supplementary marking in the form of a letter N (Nacht – night) painted on the fuselage in black with a white border.

Interesting and unusual in other air forces, was the marking of propeller spinners as a means of ideality. At the beginning of World War II they were painted in black-green (RLM 70) in the factory. In the units spinner noses, or the whole spinners, were painted in squadron colours. Sometimes coloured bands were used as in case of the spinners of Messerschmitt Bf 109s from 3./JG 21 during the period of fighting over Poland in 1939. In 1940 a quarter of the conical surface of black-green spinners was painted in squadron colours, and many aircraft during the Battle of Britain had spinners painted this way. The rotation of the propeller and spinner, caused a characteristic optical effect the purpose of which was probably to distract the aim of enemy gunners.

Arado 196A floatplane, T3+EM of "Bismarck" warship in 'maritime' RLM 73/72/65 camouflage. On the fuselage is the old type Balkenkreuz with narrow arms, even though the photo was taken at the turn of 1940. The "Bismarck" aircraft sported emblem of a white seahorse in a blue field.

(R. Michulec coll.)

Also during the late Battle of Britain period in the autumn of 1940, a supplementary identification systems in the form of yellow or white painted engine cowlings, tails or wing tips was introduced. Typical of such markings was the Messerschmitt Bf 109 E–4 of the famous Major Helmut Wick on which the spinner, engine cowling and lower part of the fin were painted in yellow (RLM 04). Aircraft of JG 54, JG 26 and JG 51 also had yellow noses and fins, while similar areas in white was characteristic for Messerschmitts of JG 3.

MARKINGS FOR TWIN ENGINED FIGHTERS

Before World War II all Luftwaffe twin engined fighters were given a four-letter military code for identification of the aircraft within the squadron, wing and

Above: An example of pre-war camouflage of RLM 63/62/61/65 on a Hs 123 A (W.Nr 2732) of one of the training assault units in 1943, five years after the painting scheme was abandoned. The black factory code of KB+QA was given an additional '8' in the unit. The Balkenkreuz has proportions of 1940 (wide white elements), small white W.Nr. 2732 above the swastika on tail. *(P. Jarrett via B. Ketley)*

Below: The process of applying a cross (Balkenkreuz) on the fuselage of a Ju 87B bomber on the assembly line of Junkers' works. Balkenkreuz has wide white elements which proves the photograph was taken after 1939. *(MVT via M. Krzyżan)*

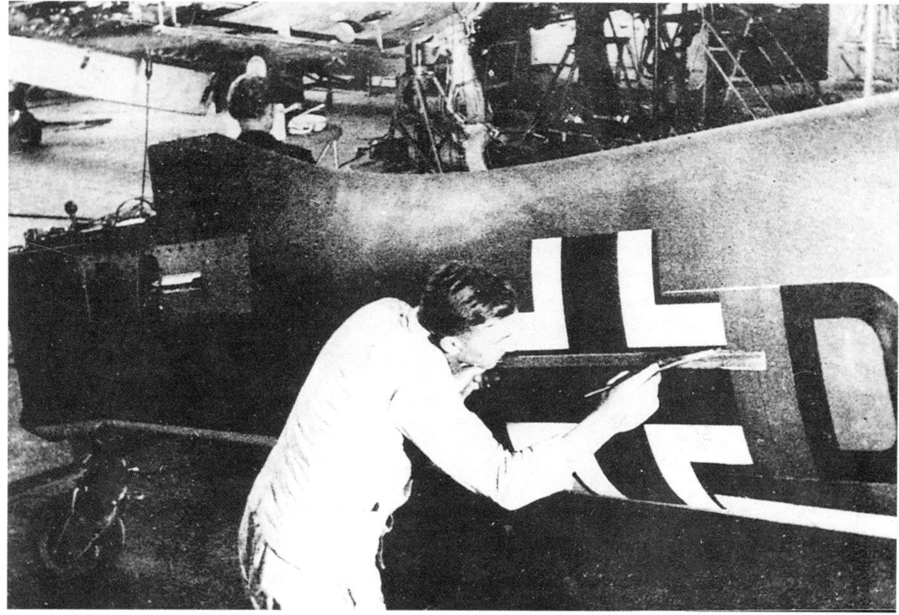

group. For example in 1940, during French Campaign a Messerschmitt Bf 110 C wore the code '3M' on the fuselage; that code indicated that the aircraft belonged to ZG 2 (Zerstörergeschwader 2). It was painted on both sides of the fuselage in black to the left of the cross. To the right of the cross, an individual aircraft letter was painted in the squadron colour (e.g. 'E'). If it was a dark colour, e.g. red on the dark green background camouflage, the letter was given a white border to render it more obvious.

White letters were used on aircraft in 1, 4, 10 and 13 squadrons; red letters in 2, 5, 8, 11 and 14 squadrons; yellow in 3, 6, 9, 12 and 15 squadrons and green letters in Wing Staff Flights (Gruppen Stab Kette); blue was characteristic for Group Staff Flights (Geschwader Stab Kette).

Beside the individual letter was painted a black letter designating both the wing and squadron; e.g. 'K'. The letter 'K' was used to identify aircraft belonging to the 2nd Squadron of ZG2, the 2nd Squadron belonging to the Ist Wing of that Group. So the third letter had a double role – it identified the squadron and the wing to which the aircraft belonged. Letters in the squadron colour doubled that, information and defined the individual position of the aircraft in the wing and squadron, as each aircraft had a different letter, and its colour designated the squadron to which it belonged.

Each group had between 9 and 15 squadrons. Each squadron had a different

The moment of Do 18 catapult take-off. The small crosses on the upper wing surface are visible, as are traces of the large additional crosses, closer to the fuselage. In a certain period the aircraft carried no less than four crosses on upper wing surface. *(R. Michulec coll.)*

A modern multi-role floatplane He 115C–1, M2+BL, of 3./KüFlGr 106 in the Summer of 1940 bore camouflage of RLM 73/72/22 – the undersurfaces, cross on the fuselage and 'B' individual letter were overpainted in black – note the careless style of the paint job. *(P. Jarrett via B. Ketley)*

identity letter; 1st Squadron – H, 2nd Squadron – K, 3rd Squadron – L, 4th Squadron – M, 5th Squadron – N, 6th Squadron – P, 7th Squadron – R, 8th Squadron – S, 9th Squadron – T, 10th Squadron – U, 11th Squadron – V, 12th Squadron – W, 13th Squadron – X, 14th Squadron – Y, 15th Squadron – Z. Aircraft of Group Staff Flights (Geschwader Stab Kette) had a letter A, and those of Wing Staff Flights (Gruppen Stab Kette) had: Ist wing – B, IInd wing – C, IIIrd wing – D, IVth wing – E, and Vth wing – F. That code, as well as appearing on the fuselage, was repeated on the underside of the wings. Under the right wing appeared the group code in black e.g. '3M' ('3' to the left of rhe cross and 'M' to the right. Under the left wing, the last two letters of code were painted with individual letter (in black) to the left of the cross, and the squadron letter to the right. It sometimes happened that markings on the underside were simplified and only the individual letter code was painted to the left of the cross under both wings and the squadron letter to the right of the cross. On many aircraft simplification were too far – only an individual letter was painted to the left or right side of the cross under the wings. The same letter was repeated in the squadron colour near the crosses on the upper wings.

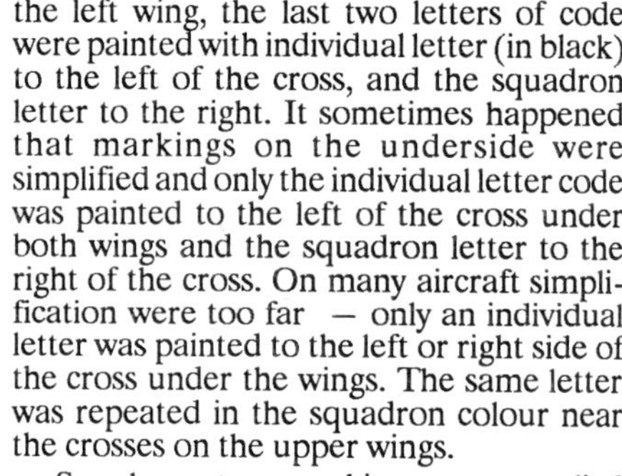

Supplementary markings were applied as with single-engined fighters, for quick identification. For example a Messerschmitt Bf 110s of ZG 26 during the Battle of Britain period in 1940 had noses and spinners painted in white. But in ZG 76 an decoration in the form of a shark mouth was painted on the noses of its Bf 110s. Spinners were painted according to the standard – all or partly painted in squadron colours.

Group attachment was defined by unit insignia, generally painted on the fuselage near the cockpit or on the nose, the designes of which were based on heraldic, animals and grotesque motifs.

MARKINGS FOR BOMBERS, RECONNAISSANCE, TRANSPORT AND TRAINING AIRCRAFT

Before any official statement of the Luftwaffe's existence, all military aircraft

A He 115 B–0, VF+UY in 'maritime' RLM 73/72/22 camouflage. *(A. Jarski coll.)*

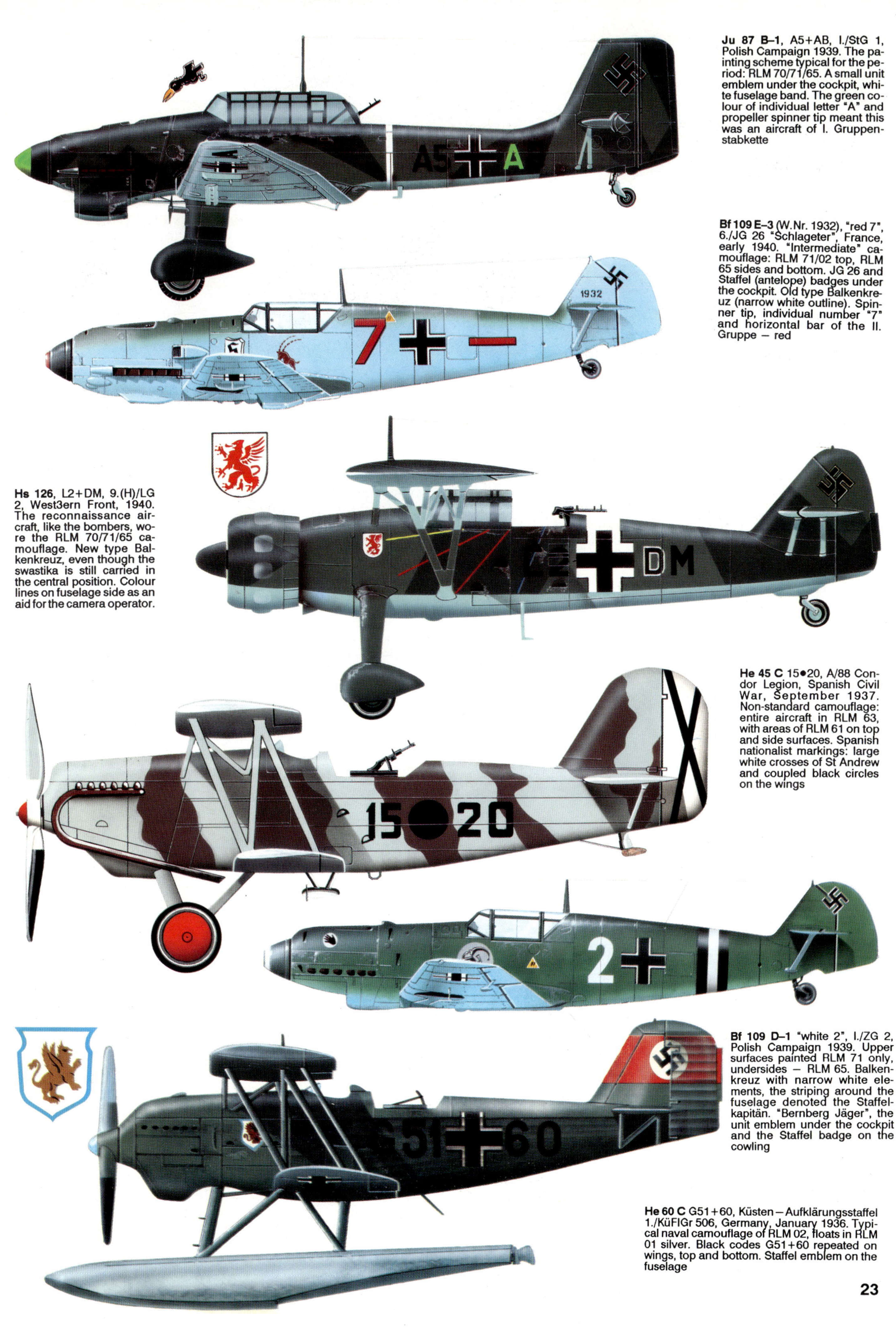

Ju 87 B–1, A5+AB, I./StG 1, Polish Campaign 1939. The painting scheme typical for the period: RLM 70/71/65. A small unit emblem under the cockpit, white fuselage band. The green colour of individual letter "A" and propeller spinner tip meant this was an aircraft of I. Gruppenstabkette

Bf 109 E–3 (W.Nr. 1932), "red 7", 6./JG 26 "Schlageter", France, early 1940. "Intermediate" camouflage: RLM 71/02 top, RLM 65 sides and bottom. JG 26 and Staffel (antelope) badges under the cockpit. Old type Balkenkreuz (narrow white outline). Spinner tip, individual number "7" and horizontal bar of the II. Gruppe – red

Hs 126, L2+DM, 9.(H)/LG 2, West3ern Front, 1940. The reconnaissance aircraft, like the bombers, wore the RLM 70/71/65 camouflage. New type Balkenkreuz, even though the swastika is still carried in the central position. Colour lines on fuselage side as an aid for the camera operator.

He 45 C 15●20, A/88 Condor Legion, Spanish Civil War, September 1937. Non-standard camouflage: entire aircraft in RLM 63, with areas of RLM 61 on top and side surfaces. Spanish nationalist markings: large white crosses of St Andrew and coupled black circles on the wings

Bf 109 D–1 "white 2", I./ZG 2, Polish Campaign 1939. Upper surfaces painted RLM 71 only, undersides – RLM 65. Balkenkreuz with narrow white elements, the striping around the fuselage denoted the Staffelkapitän. "Bernberg Jäger", the unit emblem under the cockpit and the Staffel badge on the cowling

He 60 C G51+60, Küsten – Aufklärungsstaffel 1./KüFlGr 506, Germany, January 1936. Typical naval camouflage of RLM 02, floats in RLM 01 silver. Black codes G51+60 repeated on wings, top and bottom. Staffel emblem on the fuselage

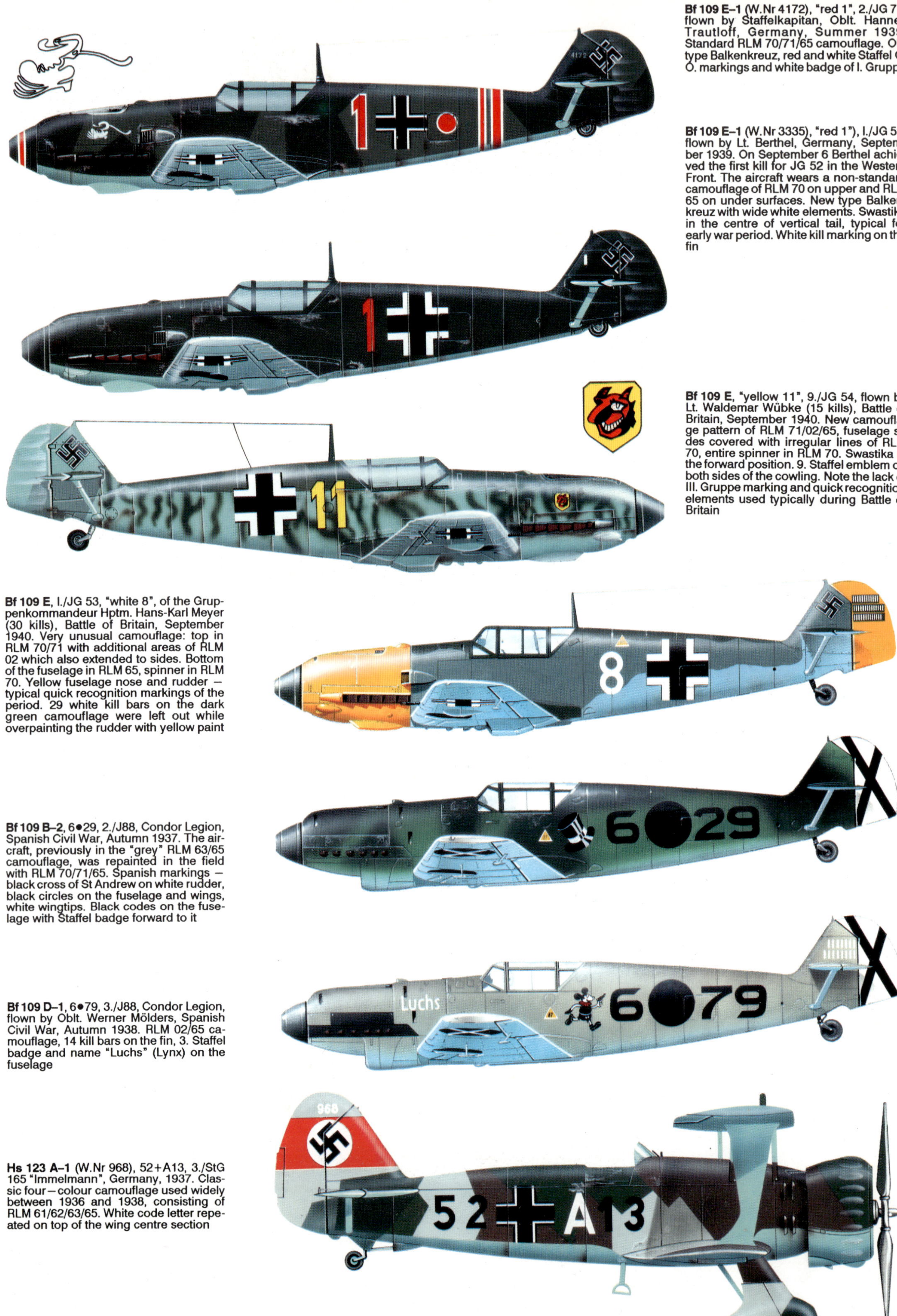

Bf 109 E–1 (W.Nr 4172), "red 1", 2./JG 77, flown by Staffelkapitan, Oblt. Hannes Trautloff, Germany, Summer 1939. Standard RLM 70/71/65 camouflage. Old type Balkenkreuz, red and white Staffel C. O. markings and white badge of I. Gruppe

Bf 109 E–1 (W.Nr 3335), "red 1"), I./JG 52, flown by Lt. Berthel, Germany, September 1939. On September 6 Berthel achieved the first kill for JG 52 in the Western Front. The aircraft wears a non-standard camouflage of RLM 70 on upper and RLM 65 on under surfaces. New type Balkenkreuz with wide white elements. Swastika in the centre of vertical tail, typical for early war period. White kill marking on the fin

Bf 109 E, "yellow 11", 9./JG 54, flown by Lt. Waldemar Wübke (15 kills), Battle of Britain, September 1940. New camouflage pattern of RLM 71/02/65, fuselage sides covered with irregular lines of RLM 70, entire spinner in RLM 70. Swastika in the forward position. 9. Staffel emblem on both sides of the cowling. Note the lack of III. Gruppe marking and quick recognition elements used typically during Battle of Britain

Bf 109 E, I./JG 53, "white 8", of the Gruppenkommandeur Hptm. Hans-Karl Meyer (30 kills), Battle of Britain, September 1940. Very unusual camouflage: top in RLM 70/71 with additional areas of RLM 02 which also extended to sides. Bottom of the fuselage in RLM 65, spinner in RLM 70. Yellow fuselage nose and rudder – typical quick recognition markings of the period. 29 white kill bars on the dark green camouflage were left out while overpainting the rudder with yellow paint

Bf 109 B–2, 6●29, 2./J88, Condor Legion, Spanish Civil War, Autumn 1937. The aircraft, previously in the "grey" RLM 63/65 camouflage, was repainted in the field with RLM 70/71/65. Spanish markings – black cross of St Andrew on white rudder, black circles on the fuselage and wings, white wingtips. Black codes on the fuselage with Staffel badge forward to it

Bf 109 D–1, 6●79, 3./J88, Condor Legion, flown by Oblt. Werner Mölders, Spanish Civil War, Autumn 1938. RLM 02/65 camouflage, 14 kill bars on the fin, 3. Staffel badge and name "Luchs" (Lynx) on the fuselage

Hs 123 A–1 (W.Nr 968), 52+A13, 3./StG 165 "Immelmann", Germany, 1937. Classic four–colour camouflage used widely between 1936 and 1938, consisting of RLM 61/62/63/65. White code letter repeated on top of the wing centre section

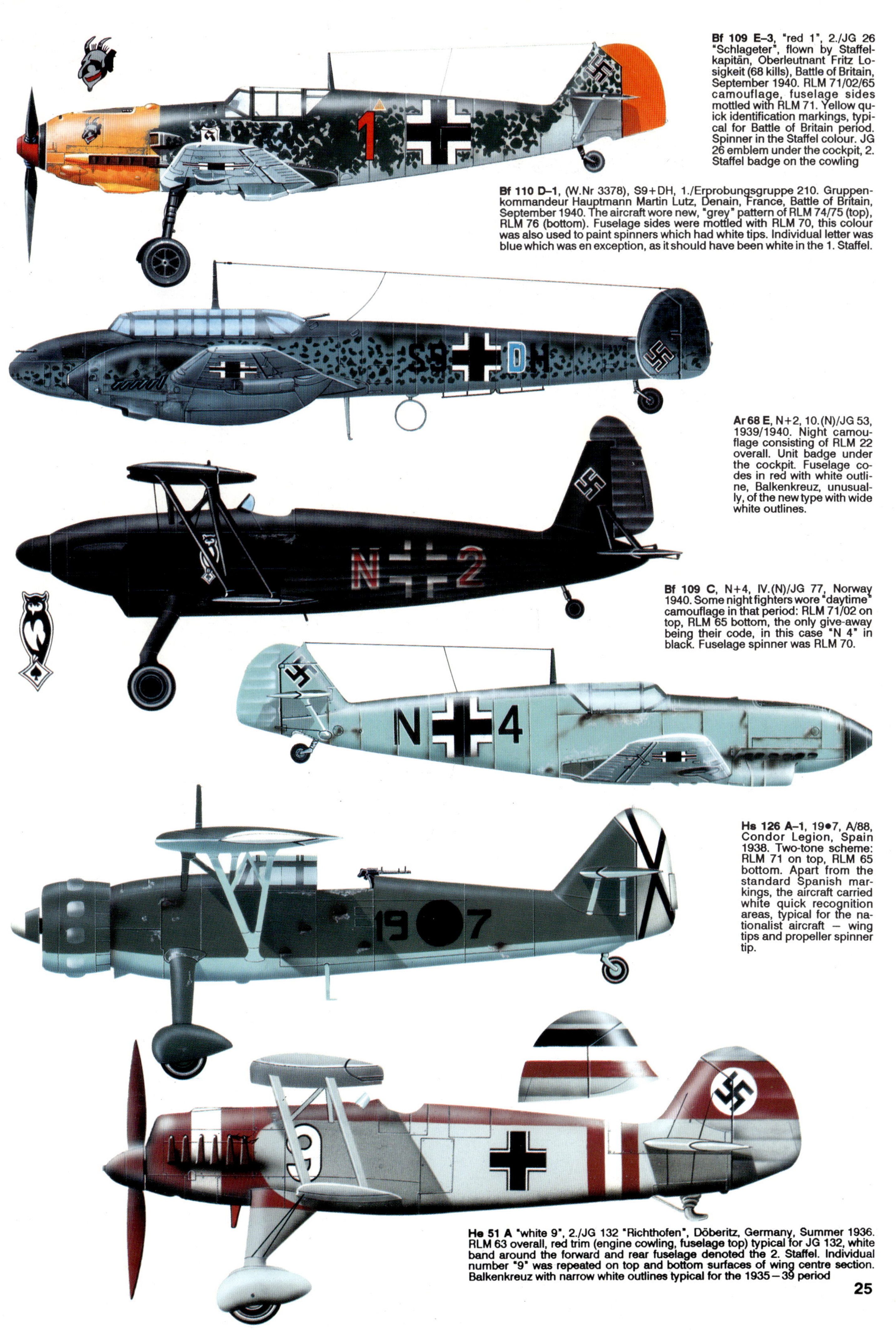

Bf 109 E–3, "red 1", 2./JG 26 "Schlageter", flown by Staffelkapitän, Oberleutnant Fritz Losigkeit (68 kills), Battle of Britain, September 1940. RLM 71/02/65 camouflage, fuselage sides mottled with RLM 71. Yellow quick identification markings, typical for Battle of Britain period. Spinner in the Staffel colour. JG 26 emblem under the cockpit, 2. Staffel badge on the cowling

Bf 110 D–1, (W.Nr 3378), S9+DH, 1./Erprobungsgruppe 210. Gruppenkommandeur Hauptmann Martin Lutz, Denain, France, Battle of Britain, September 1940. The aircraft wore new, "grey" pattern of RLM 74/75 (top), RLM 76 (bottom). Fuselage sides were mottled with RLM 70, this colour was also used to paint spinners which had white tips. Individual letter was blue which was en exception, as it should have been white in the 1. Staffel.

Ar 68 E, N+2, 10.(N)/JG 53, 1939/1940. Night camouflage consisting of RLM 22 overall. Unit badge under the cockpit. Fuselage codes in red with white outline, Balkenkreuz, unusually, of the new type with wide white outlines.

Bf 109 C, N+4, IV.(N)/JG 77, Norway 1940. Some night fighters wore "daytime" camouflage in that period: RLM 71/02 on top, RLM 65 bottom, the only give-away being their code, in this case "N 4" in black. Fuselage spinner was RLM 70.

Hs 126 A–1, 19•7, A/88, Condor Legion, Spain 1938. Two-tone scheme: RLM 71 on top, RLM 65 bottom. Apart from the standard Spanish markings, the aircraft carried white quick recognition areas, typical for the nationalist aircraft – wing tips and propeller spinner tip.

He 51 A "white 9", 2./JG 132 "Richthofen", Döberitz, Germany, Summer 1936. RLM 63 overall, red trim (engine cowling, fuselage top) typical for JG 132, white band around the forward and rear fuselage denoted the 2. Staffel. Individual number "9" was repeated on top and bottom surfaces of wing centre section. Balkenkreuz with narrow white outlines typical for the 1935–39 period

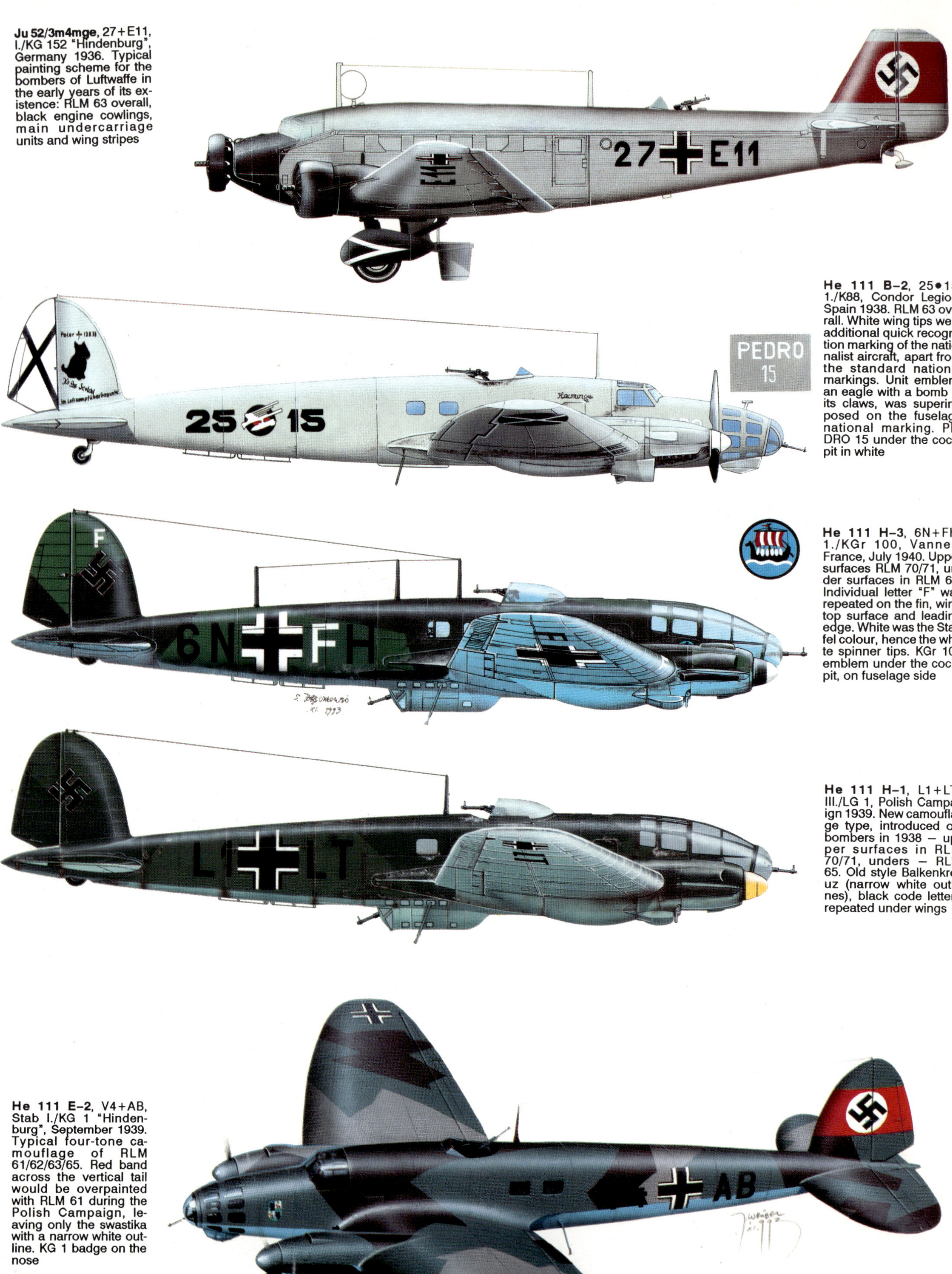

Ju 52/3m4mge, 27+E11, I./KG 152 "Hindenburg", Germany 1936. Typical painting scheme for the bombers of Luftwaffe in the early years of its existence: RLM 63 overall, black engine cowlings, main undercarriage units and wing stripes

He 111 B-2, 25•15, 1./K88, Condor Legion, Spain 1938. RLM 63 overall. White wing tips were additional quick recognition marking of the nationalist aircraft, apart from the standard national markings. Unit emblem, an eagle with a bomb in its claws, was superimposed on the fuselage national marking. PEDRO 15 under the cockpit in white

He 111 H-3, 6N+FH, 1./KGr 100, Vannes, France, July 1940. Upper surfaces RLM 70/71, under surfaces in RLM 65. Individual letter "F" was repeated on the fin, wing top surface and leading edge. White was the Staffel colour, hence the white spinner tips. KGr 100 emblem under the cockpit, on fuselage side

He 111 H-1, L1+LT, III./LG 1, Polish Campaign 1939. New camouflage type, introduced on bombers in 1938 – upper surfaces in RLM 70/71, unders – RLM 65. Old style Balkenkreuz (narrow white outlines), black code letters repeated under wings

He 111 E-2, V4+AB, Stab I./KG 1 "Hindenburg", September 1939. Typical four-tone camouflage of RLM 61/62/63/65. Red band across the vertical tail would be overpainted with RLM 61 during the Polish Campaign, leaving only the swastika with a narrow white outline. KG 1 badge on the nose

Above: Bf 109E–4 'red 4' of II/JG 2 "Richthofen", France, 1940. The aircraft bears a non-standard camouflage pattern – originally the fuselage sides were blue (RLM 65), and the fuselage top was in RLM 71 and 02. Then the sides of the fuselage were brush-painted with RLM 71 paint. This was a provisional camouflage applied to aircraft based at airfields in France, where they were often 'visited' by allied bombers.

(P. Jarrett via B. Ketley)

had registration numbers painted in black on the fuselage sides and on the wings. Prior to the April 1934, registration number consisted of the letter 'D' and four numbers after a dash, but after that time the dash was removed and four letters replaced the previously used numbers.

As the national markings on the fin were introduced, tactical numbers in black were often painted on the fuselage and wings in addition – to the civil registrations numbers. In the autumn of 1935, with the introduction of national insignia in form of the cross, five digit military codes (e.g. 52+E26) had been painted on Luftwaffe aircraft. The first character indicaded the Air District (Luftkreis), the second character the Group number (Geschwader), the third was an individual, the fourth and fifth indicated the Wing (Gruppe) and Squadron (Staffel) respectively.

For example the code 32+A25 painted on the Do 23 G bomber means:
3 – Luftkreiskommando III, Dresden
2 – second Group (Geschwader) in Air District
A – aircraft 'A' in the squadron

Above: A Bf 109E with non–standard markings of the JG 26 Gruppenadjutant on the fuselage – black horizontal bar with a letter 'A' in white outline. Camouflage RLM 02/71/65 typical for the early war period on the Western Front in 1940.

(MVT via M. Krzyżan)

A reconnaissance Hs 126 during an overhaul. RLM 70/71/65 camouflage. Balkenkreuz of the pre-war type, well visible typical wing tip position for the early-style cross, later – since 1940 – they were applied closer to the fuselage.

(Z. Titz via R. L. Ward)

Above: Another shot of a II./ZG 76 Bf 110 C shows well the way the sharkmouth was painted on the nose. Two last characters of the code are visible on the fuselage. The red 'B' is outlined in white — red was the colour of the 5. Staffel, as confirmed by the black 'N'. The typical sharkmouth enables identification of the remaining part of the code — 'M8' for the II. Gruppe of ZG 76. Two flags on the fuselage, the Belgian and the French ones, mark the two campaigns fought by the aircraft.

(P. Jarrett via B. Ketley)

The famous Stuka — star of Blietzkrieg. A Junkers Ju 87B–1 of I/StG 1 (1939). 'Green' camouflage of RLM 70/71/65, typical for early years of war. Balkenkreuz on the fuselage has narrow white elements. In 1940 a new type of cross was introduced which featured wider white portions. White individual letter was repeated on top and bottom surface of the wings. Also the propeller spinner tip was white (white was the colour of 1. Staffel). *(MVT via M. Krzyżan)*

2 — II Gruppe (IInd Wing)
5 — 5 Staffel (5th Squadron).

Some differences exist in the case of naval aircraft markings; because there were no special or separate naval aviation groups, the second number in the code was replaced by '0'.

For example the code 60+U51 on a He 114 from 1./KuFlGr 506 means:
6 — Luftkreiscommando VI, Kiel
0 — naval aviation aircraft
U — aircraft „U" in the Wing
5 — 5 Gruppe (5th Wing)
1 — 1 Staffel (1st Squadron).

A Do 26 V–4 flying boat, P5+DH, serving in KGr.zb.V. 108 during the Norwegian Campaign in 1940. Aircraft in the 'maritime' camouflage of RLM 73/72/65. 1940-standard Balkenkreuzes (wide white areas). *(MVT via M. Krzyżan)*

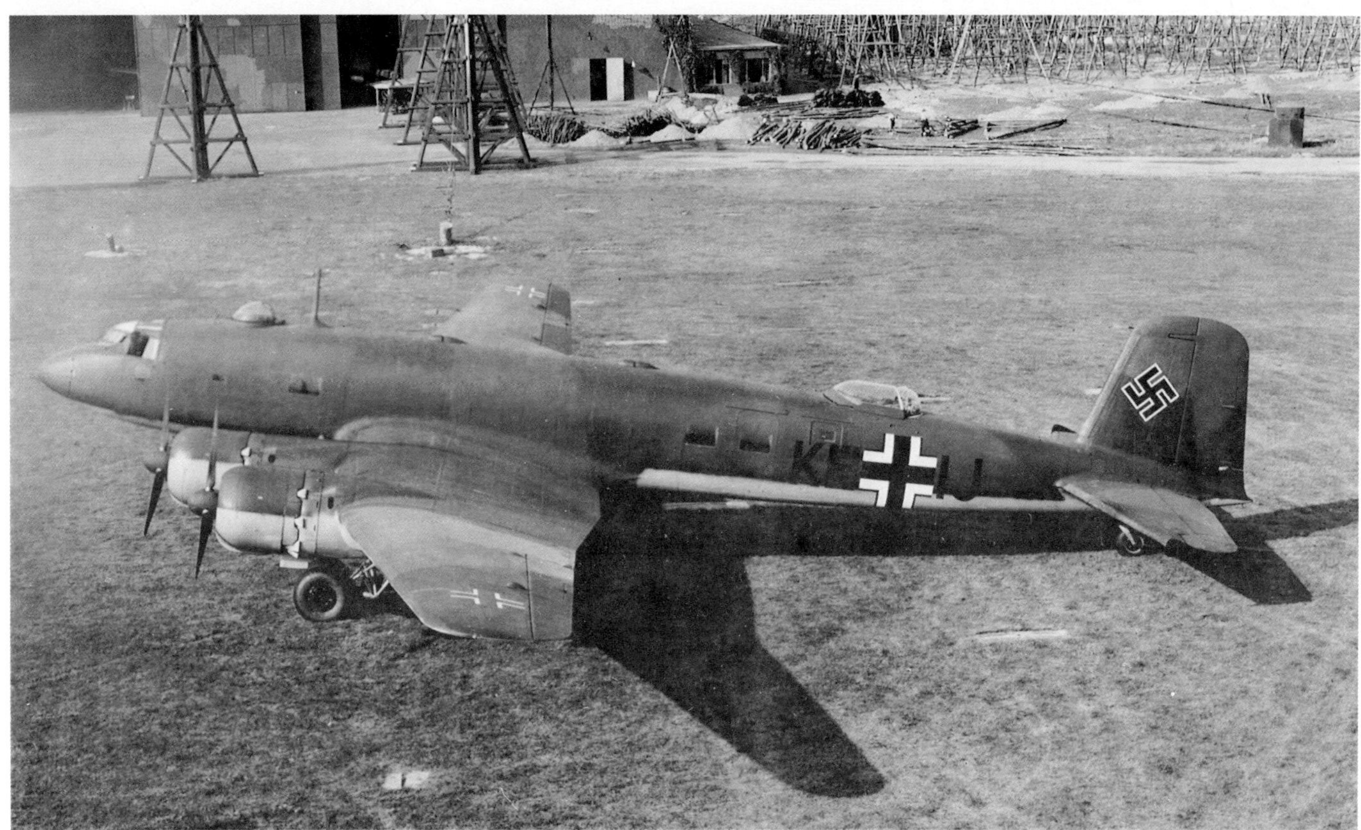

Above: Dangerous enemy of the allied convoys – the Fw 200 C-3 "Condor", KE+IV, in the typical 'sea' camouflage of RLM 72/73/65.
(MVT via M. Krzyżan)

Before World War II (end of 1938 or early of 1939) these codes were reduced to four symbols, painted in black on the fuselage and wings. The first two characters were a coded group number and were always painted to the left of fuselage cross and on the underside of right wing in the order: number – cross – number. In the third position in the code sequence was the individual aircraft letter, painted in the squadron colour and always to the right of the fuselage's cross and in black on the underside of left wing on the left side of the cross. Sometimes individual letters were repeated in the squadron colour on the upper wings near to the crosses. Sometimes on the undersides there were only the individual letters at both wing tips. The fourth character in the code identified a particular squadron number in the group according to rule: H – 1. Squadron, K – 2. Squadron, L – 3. Squadron, M – 4. Squadron, N – 5. Squadron, P – 6. Squadron, R – 7. Squadron, S – 8. Squadron, T – 9. Squadron, U – 10. Squadron, V – 11. Squadron, W – 12. Squadron, X – 13. Squadron, Y – 14. Squadron, Z – 15. Squadron, A – Group Staff Flight (Geschwaderstab Kette), B – Ist Wing Staff Flight (Gruppenstab Kette), C – IInd Wing Staff Flight, D – IIIrd Wing Staff Flight, E – IVth Wing Staff Flight, F – Vth Wing Staff Flight.

Two photos of a He 111P, G1+FA of Geschwaderstab KG 55 "Greif" shot down over England, summer 1940. The swastika painted on the central part of tail surface (typical 1938–39) while the fuselage Balkenkreuz is of the new type (of 1940). On the fuselage the Geschwader emblem can be seen behind the cockpit. Letter 'F' was green with white outline. Camouflage RLM 70/71/65.
(both M. D. Howley via R. L. Ward)

Supplementary markings, making for easier identification of the unit, included the system of painting spinners; most often they were painted all or partly in the squadron colour, and sometimes in addition the spinner nose was painted in the Wing colour. Each wing (Gruppe) in the group had a colour that was the background colour of the group emblem shield: I Gruppe – white, II Gruppe – red, III Gruppe – yellow, IV Gruppe – blue, V Gruppe black. Group insignia were painted generally near the cockpit. As a general rule the group insignia was a colourful figurative drawing placed on the shield background. Sometimes the shield had a border, which colour identified a squadron: white – 1., 4., 10. and 13.; red – 2., 5., 8., 11. and 14.; yellow – 3., 6., 9., 12. and 15. This system was generally applied from the beginning of the war; it was not strictly adhered to, and in some units aircraft had no group insignia at all, or each wing in the group had individual insignia – in which case both group and wing insignia were applied.

During 1939–1940, a large number of supplementary markings had been used, units commanders aircraft had narrow white bands around the mid-fuselage position (most often painted on Dornier 17s), and also white bars painted on the fins and on the upper wings. The number of these bars depended on which Staff Flight in the group it belonged to. One bar meant Ist Wing, two bars – IInd Wing, three bars – IIIrd Wing. It made for easier identification of the aircraft in the formations during operations.

A separate matter is the markings of the training aircraft. After the introduction of the letter – number code system in all training aircraft recieved proper markings. These consisted of the letter S (Schule – training), the number of Air District (1–6), a letter that indicated a particular aviation school, and the individual aircraft number in that school. For example two Bf 109Bs from an air school in the IInd Air District wore the markings S2+M57 and S2+M58. This markings system was used in multi-engine aircraft pilots schools, the so called C-Schule, and there are also known photographs of the basic training aircraft e.g. an Arado Ar 66 with the marking S2+V12. The following are examples of such markings:

Dornier Do 15 Militär Wal from FFS Settin school, July 1939 (RLM 02 scheme) with the marking S6+B76.

Heinkel He 46 with the marking S2+A35 from Sch./FAR (long range reconnaissance school) in Neustad – Gleve, August 1938 (RLM 61/62/63/65 scheme).

Heinkel He 46, S7+J37, from FFS(B) school in Oldenburg, May 1939 (RLM 63), Aero Ab 101, S7+B103, from Sch./FAR 33 in Ingolstadt.

Shortly before the war started new registration numbers were introduced, with the letters WL in place of Air District markings. Anexample of such was Hs 123 WL+IPNC from Sch./FAR 41 school in Frankfurt on Oder.

Marking training and utility aircraft with the letters 'WL' was used until March 1940. Later, radio codes were introduced; each school received a two-letter block, for example the school in Prague had the letters PF, e.g. code letters PF+OD on a Gotha Go 145. Apart from this marking training aircraft often had supplementary numbers

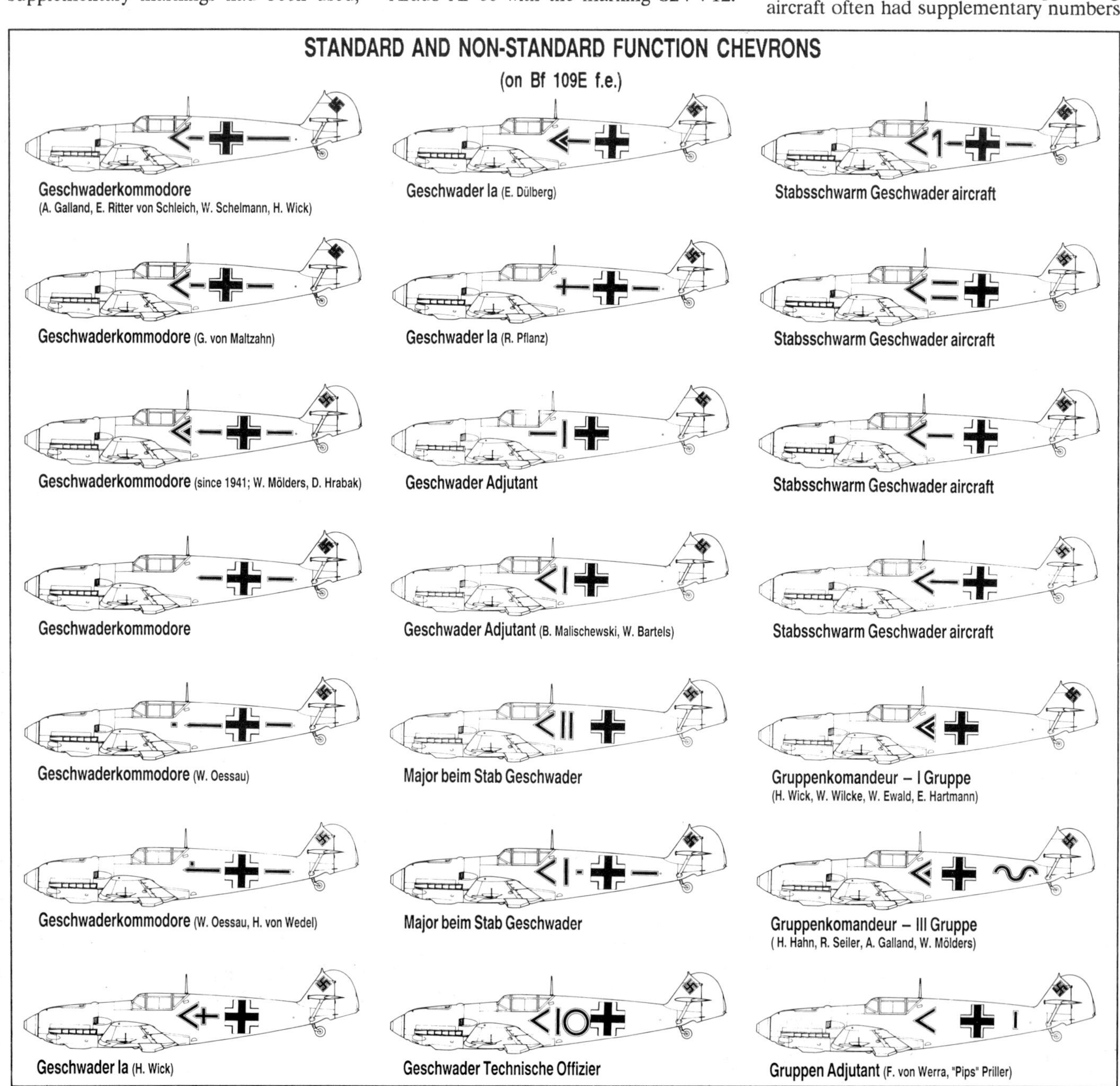

STANDARD AND NON-STANDARD FUNCTION CHEVRONS

(on Bf 109E f.e.)

Geschwaderkommodore (A. Galland, E. Ritter von Schleich, W. Schelmann, H. Wick)

Geschwader Ia (E. Dülberg)

Stabsschwarm Geschwader aircraft

Geschwaderkommodore (G. von Maltzahn)

Geschwader Ia (R. Pflanz)

Stabsschwarm Geschwader aircraft

Geschwaderkommodore (since 1941; W. Mölders, D. Hrabak)

Geschwader Adjutant

Stabsschwarm Geschwader aircraft

Geschwaderkommodore

Geschwader Adjutant (B. Malischewski, W. Bartels)

Stabsschwarm Geschwader aircraft

Geschwaderkommodore (W. Oessau)

Major beim Stab Geschwader

Gruppenkomandeur – I Gruppe (H. Wick, W. Wilcke, W. Ewald, E. Hartmann)

Geschwaderkommodore (W. Oessau, H. von Wedel)

Major beim Stab Geschwader

Gruppenkomandeur – III Gruppe (H. Hahn, R. Seiler, A. Galland, W. Mölders)

Geschwader Ia (H. Wick)

Geschwader Technische Offizier

Gruppen Adjutant (F. von Werra, "Pips" Priller)

painted or on the fuselage or engine cowlings of multi-engine types and on the wings.

Ju 52/3Ms in units used for the airborne training of parachutists had registrations numbers according to the rules used in 1935–36, and the aircraft were painted in the 61/62/63/65 camouflage. An example was S5+C28 from the Fürth school.

INDIVIDUAL INSIGNIA AND VICTORY SYMBOLS

Individualism has a deep roots in the traditions. This was sometimes displayed in the form of extra emblems, insignia or inscriptions painted on the aircraft by pilots, gunners. World War I traditions (which incorporated much of the heraldry and ethos of the knights of old) had a spectacular influence in the creation of the individual

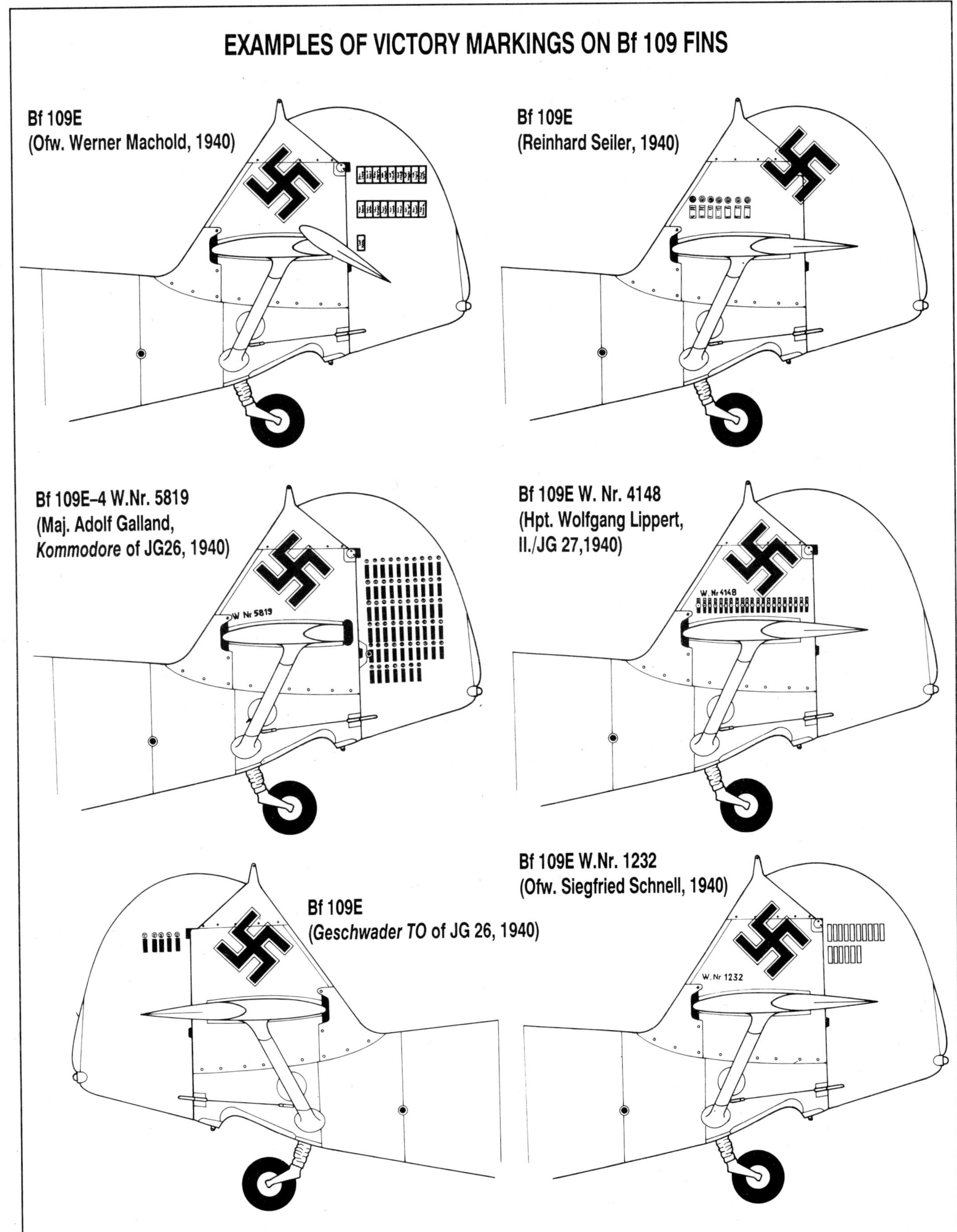

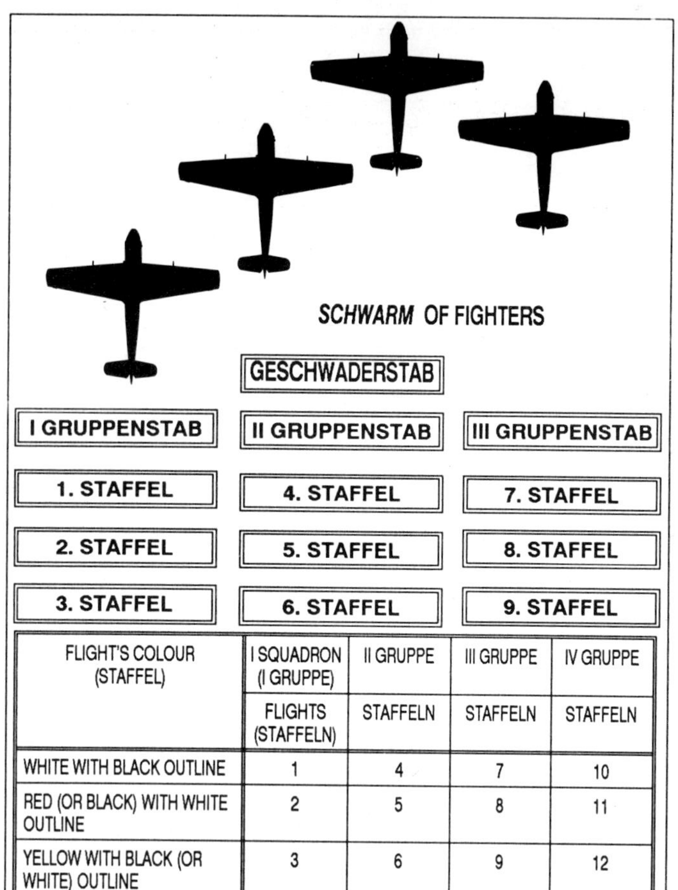

FLIGHT'S COLOUR (STAFFEL)	I SQUADRON (I GRUPPE)	II GRUPPE	III GRUPPE	IV GRUPPE
	FLIGHTS (STAFFELN)	STAFFELN	STAFFELN	STAFFELN
WHITE WITH BLACK OUTLINE	1	4	7	10
RED (OR BLACK) WITH WHITE OUTLINE	2	5	8	11
YELLOW WITH BLACK (OR WHITE) OUTLINE	3	6	9	12

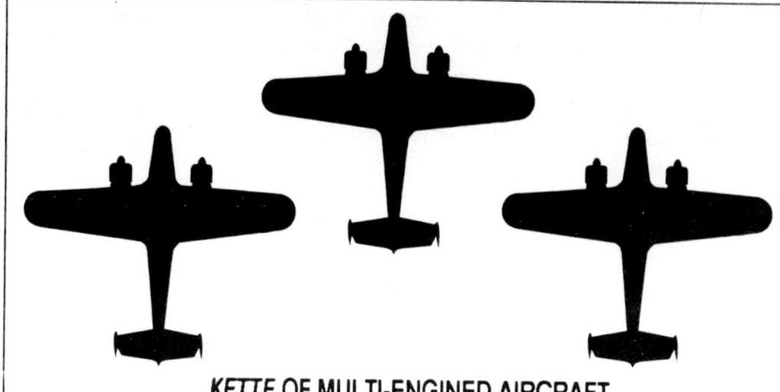

KETTE OF MULTI-ENGINED AIRCRAFT

COLOUR OF THE IDENTIFICATION LETTERS OF THE BOMBER AND DESTROYER FLIGHTS

STAFFEL (FLIGHT)	GRUPPEN (SQUADRONS)				
	I	II	III	IV	V
WHITE	1 STAFFEL - H	4 - M	7 - R	10 - U	13 - X
RED	2 STAFFEL - K	5 - N	8 - S	11 - V	14 - Y
YELLOW	3 STAFFEL - L	6 - P	9 - T	12 - W	15 - Z

COLOUR OF THE IDENTIFICATION LETTERS OF THE STAFF FLIGHTS IN BOMBER AND DESTROYER UNITS

bLUE	A - GESCHWADERSTAB
GREEN	B - IGRUPPENSTAB
GREEN	C - II GRUPPENSTAB
GREEN	D - III GRUPPENSTAB
GREEN	E - IV GRUPPENSTAB
GREEN	F - V GRUPPENSTAB

emblems and insignia used in WW II especially amongst fighter pilots. Heraldic devices, animal and other allegorical motifs were predominant inspirations for such adornments.

Besides individual insignia victory symbols were to become commonplace; for the first time they appeared on the fins of Condor Legion fighters – adjecone upright bars several centimetres in length, painted in white. Each bar stood for one victory. Probably in the same way victories during the war in Poland in 1939 would probably have been marked in the same manner; sometimes the bar was supplemented by the date of the victory painted over it in the same colour.

Later on bars in different colours were also used for example in black or red and sometimes yellow. Over the bars appeared the date of the victory, often supplemented by a small profile of the destroyed aircraft, or an allied national insignia e.g. French or British roundel.

On the fins or rudders of fighters honours gained by the pilot were also applied; these took the form of a Knight Cross (Ritterkreuz), supplemented by the number of victories for which the honour was awarded.

Generally on bombers the number of missions was not marked (unlike the bombers belonging to the allies). However small white or black profiles painted on the fins or rudders of Luftwaffe bombers indicated the destruction of particular targets (e.g. warships, tanks, cargo ships, aircraft). Such symbols were often supplemented by the date of sinking or damaging a warship or vessel, and sometimes the tonnage of enemy ship, and its nationality, as was common practice for example in KG 30 "Adler" and KG 40.

PROPORTIONS FOR AIRCRAFT LETTERS AND NUMBERS

ABCW

h

6/7 h — 5/7 h — 5/7 h — 8/7 h

ABCDEFG
HIJKLMNO
PQRSTUV
WXYZÖ90
12345678

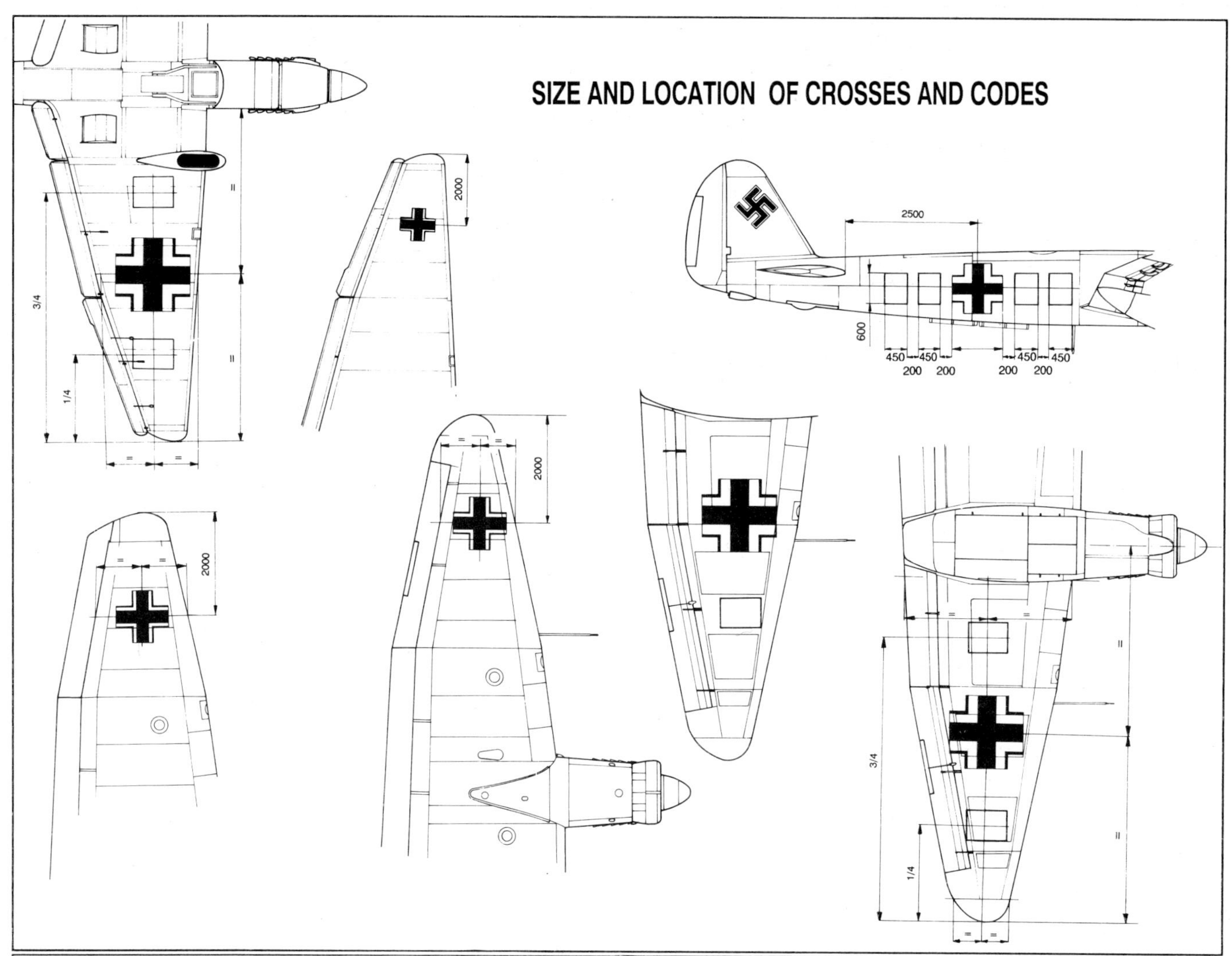

LUFTWAFFE CODE SYSTEM DURING 1935 – 39 PERIOD

CODE	UNIT	AIR DISTRICT
10+X 11/2/3/4	121. Long Range Recce Squadron (F 121)	Königsberg
10+X 21/2/3	11. Tactical Recce Squadron (H 11)	
20+X 1/2/2	Reconnaissance Squadron	Berlin
20+X 11/2/3	122. Long Range Recce Squadron (F 122)	
20+X 21/2/3	12. Tactical Recce Squadron (H 12)	
20+X 31/2/3	52. Tactical Recce Squadron (H 52)	
21+X 11/2/3	I. Squadron of 132. Fighter Regiment (I(JG 132)	
21+X 21/2/3	II.Squadron of 132. Fighter Regiment (II./JG 132)	
21+X 31/2/3	III. Squadron of 132. Fighter Regiment (III./JG 132)	
21+X 41/2/3	IV. Squadron of 132. Fighter Regiment (IV./JG 132)	
23+X 11/2/3	I. Squadron of 162. Dive Bomber Rgt (I./St.G. 162)	
23+X 24/5/6	II. Squadron of 162. Dive Bomber Regiment (II./St.G.162)	
23+X 37/8/9	III. Squadron of 162. Dive Bomber Rgt (III./St.G.162)	
25+X 11/2/3	I. Squadron of 152. Bomber Regiment (I./KG.152)	
25+X 24/5/6	II. Squadron of 152. Bomber Regiment (II./KG.152)	
25+X 37/8/9	III. Squadron of 152. Bomber Regiment (III./KG.152)	
27+X 11/2/3	I. Squadron of Bomber Regiment	
27+X 21/2/3	II. Squadron of Bomber Regiment	
27+X 31/2/3	III. Squadron of Bomber Regiment	
30+X 11/2/3	123. Long Range Recce Squadron (F 123)	Dresden
30+X 21/2/3	13. Tactical Recce Squadron (H 13)	
32+X 11/2/3	I. Squadron of 153. Bomber Regiment (I./KG 153)	
32+X 24/5/6	II. Squadron of 153. Bomber Regiment (II./KG 153)	
32+X 37/8/9	III. Squadron of 153. Bomber Regiment (III./KG 153)	
33+X 11/2/3	I. Squadron of 253. Bomber Regiment (I./KG 253)	
33+X 24/5/6	II. Squadron of 253. Bomber Regiment (II./KG 253)	
33+X 37/8/9	III. Squadron of 253. Bomber Regiment (III./KG 253)	
35+X 11/2/3	I. Squadron of 163. Dive Bomber Rgt (I./St.G. 163)	
35+X 24/2/3	II. Squadron of 163. Dive Bomber Rgt (II./St.G. 163)	
35+X 37/8/9	III. Squadron of 163. Dive Bomber Rgt (III./St.G. 163)	
40+X 11/2/3	124. Long Range Recce Squadron (F 124)	Münster
40+X 21/2/3	14. Tactical Recce Squadron (H 14)	
40+X 31/2/3	Tactical Recce Squadron (H 224 ?)	
41+X 11/2/3	I. Squadron of 154. Bomber Regiment (I./KG 154)	Münster
41+X 24/5/6	II. Squadron of 154. Bomber Regiment (II./KG 154)	
41+X 37/8/9	III. Squadron of 154. Bomber Regiment (III./KG 154)	
42+X 11/2/3	I. Squadron of 254. Bomber Regiment (I./KG 254)	
42+X 24/5/6	II. Squadron of 254.Bomber Regiment (II./KG 254)	
42+X 37/8/9	III. Squadron of 254. Bomber Regiment (III./KG 254)	
42+X 10/11/12	IV. Squadron of 254. Bomber Regiment (IV/KG 254)	
50+X11/2/3	125. Long Range Recce Squadron (F 125)	München
50+X 21/2/3/4/7	15. Tactical Recce Squadron (H 15)	
51+X 11/2/3/	I. Squadron of 135. Fighter Regiment (I./JG 135)	
52+X 11/2/3	I. Squadron of 165 Dive Bomber Rgt (I./St.G. 165)	
52+X 24/5/6	II. Squadron of 165. Dive Bomber Rgt (II./St.G. 165)	
52+X 37/8/9	III. Squadron of 165. Dive Bomber Rgt (III./St.G. 165)	
53+X 11/2/3	I. Squadron of 155. Bomber Regiment (I./KG 155)	
53+X 24/5/6	II. Squadron of 155. Bomber Regiment (II./KG 155)	
53+X 37/8/8	III. Squadron of 155. Bomber Regiment (III./KG 155)	
54+X 11/2/3	I. Squadron of 255. Bomber Regiment (I./KG 255)	
54+X 24/5/6	II. Squadron of 255. Bomber Regiment (II./KG 255)	
54+X 37/8/9	III. Squadron of 255. Bomber Regiment (III./KG 255)	
55+X 11/2/3	I. Squadron of 355. Bomber Regiment (I./KG 355)	
55+X 24/5/6	II. Squadron of 355. Bomber Regiment (II./KG 355)	
55+X 37/8/9	III. Squadron of 355. Bomber Regiment (III./KG 355)	
60+X 11/2/3	106. Coastal Recce Squadron (K 106)	Kiel
60+X 21/2/3	206. Coastal Recce Squadron (K 206)	
60+X 31/2/3	306. Coastal Recce Squadron (K 306)	
60+X 41/2/3	136. Coastal Fighter Squadron (KJG 136)	
70+X 11/2/3	127. Long Range Recce Squadron (F 127)	Braunschweig
71+X 11/2/3	I. Squadron of 157. Bomber Regiment (I./KG 157)	
71+X 24/5/6	II. Squadron of 157. Bomber Regiment (II./KG 157)	
71+X 37/8/9	III. Squadron of 157. Bomber Regiment (III./KG 157)	
72+X 11/2/3	I. Squadron of 257. Bomber Regiment (I./KG 257)	
72+X 24/5/6	II. Squadron of 257. Bomber Regiment (II./KG 257)	
72+X 37/8/9	III. Squadron of 257. Bomber Regiment (III./KG 257)	
80 +X 11/2/3	18. Reconnaissance Squadron (A 18)	Wien

X – individual aircraft letter
\+ – Balkenkreuz

Regiment = Geschwader (G), Squadron = Gruppe (Gr), Flight = Staffel (St.), Trainer = Lehr (L), Bomber = Kampf (K), Dive = Stuka (St.), Attack = Schlacht (Schl), Fighter = Jagd (J), Night = Nacht (N), Pursuit (Destroyer) = Zerstörer (Z), Reconnaissance = Aufklärungs (A), Long Recce = Fernaufklärungs (F), Tactical Recce = Heeres (H).

Standard A camouflage scheme of 1936 for the Henschel 123A–1 dive bomber. The colours used: upper surfaces RLM 61 Dunkelbraun dark brown, RLM 62 Grün green, and RLM 63 Grüngrau light grey-green; under surfaces RLM 65 Hellblau light blue. The camouflage colours could be exchanged but within the same division lines. Another scheme existed, which was a mirror image of the A scheme. Black swastika in white disc was applied on a red band on the vertical tail. The Balkenkreuz in proportions of 1936. Mainwheel spats were usually (albeit not always) painted in camouflage. Propeller blades black (rear surface) and bare metal (front), later black overall.

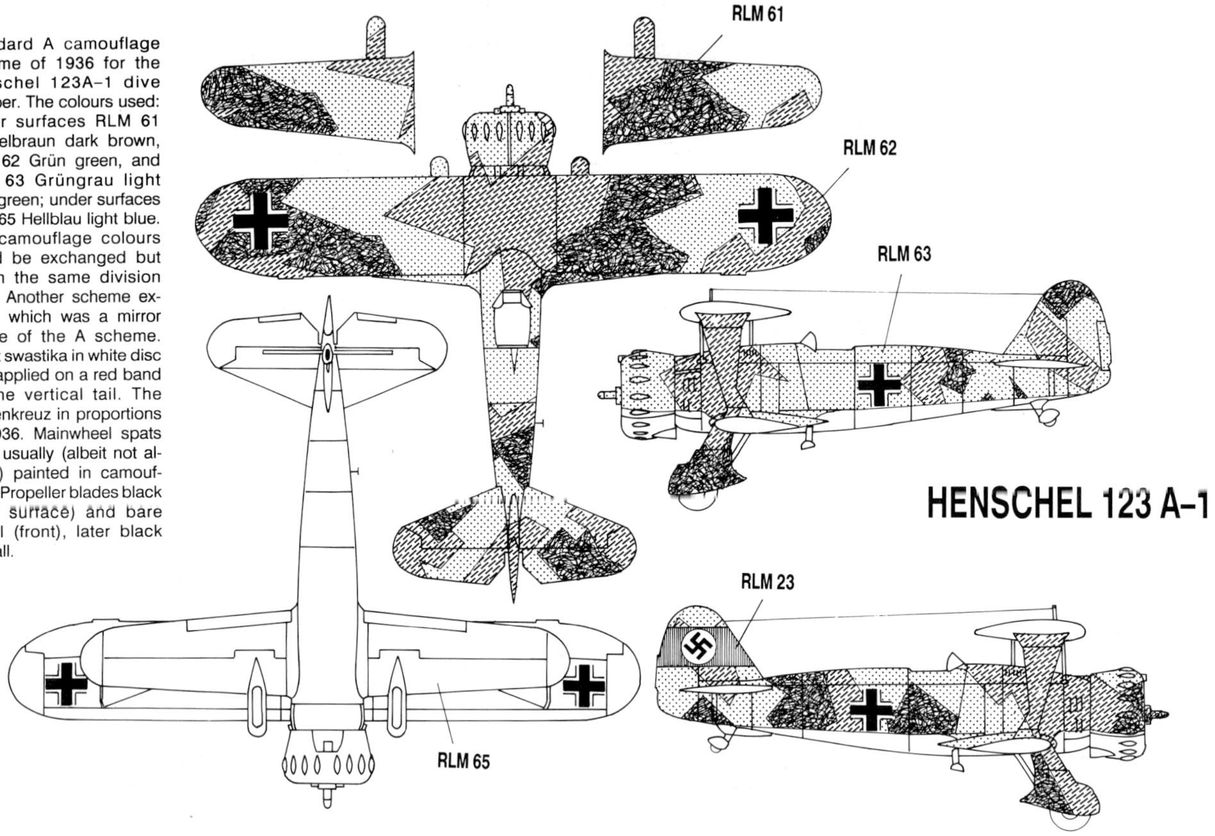

RLM 61

RLM 62

RLM 63

HENSCHEL 123 A–1

RLM 23

RLM 65

RLM 61

RLM 62

RLM 63

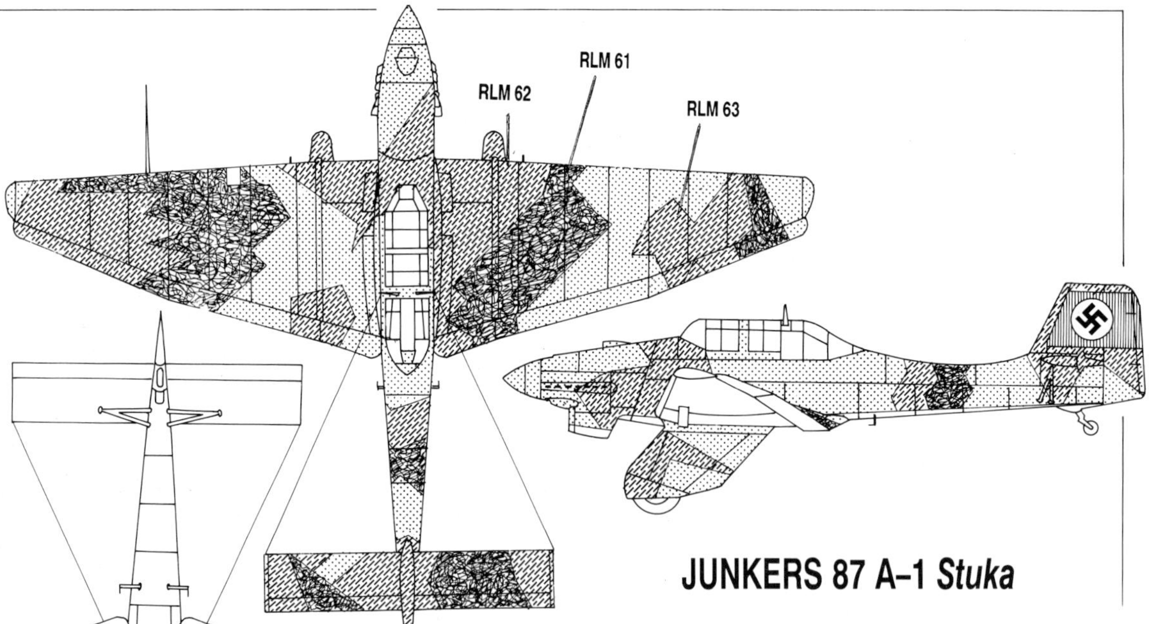

JUNKERS 87 A–1 *Stuka*

Standard A camouflage scheme of 1936 for the Junkers 87A dive bomber. The colours used: upper surfaces RLM 61 Dunkelbraun dark brown, RLM 62 Grün – green, and RLM 63 Grüngrau – light grey-green; under surfaces RLM 65 Hellblau – light blue. The camouflage colours could be exchanged but within the same division lines. Another scheme existed, which was a mirror image of the A scheme. Black swastika in white disc was applied on a red band on the vertical tail. The Balkenkreuz in proportions of 1936.

RLM 23

RLM 65

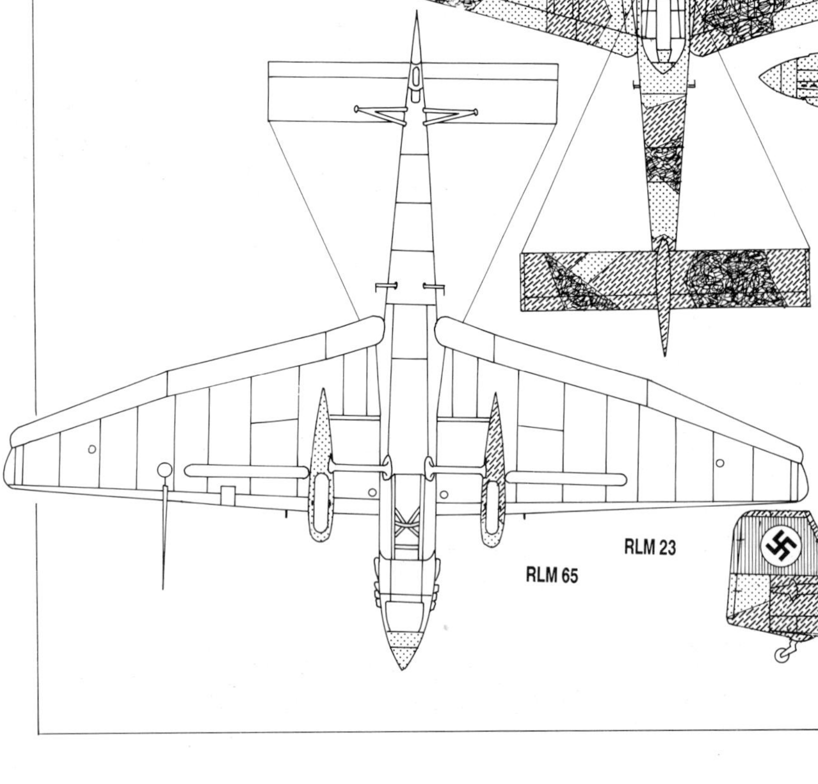

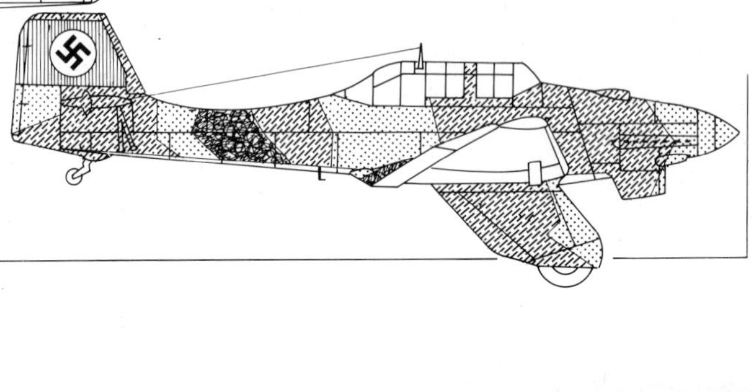

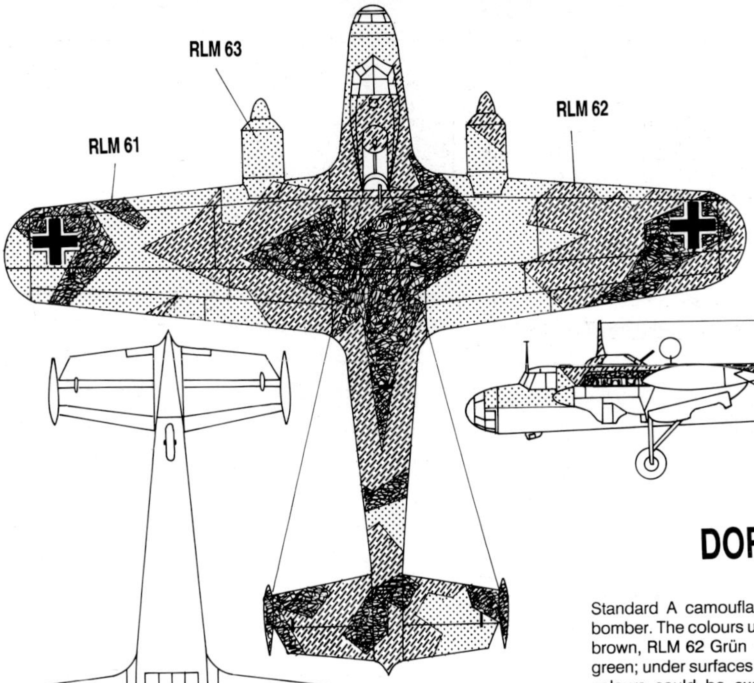

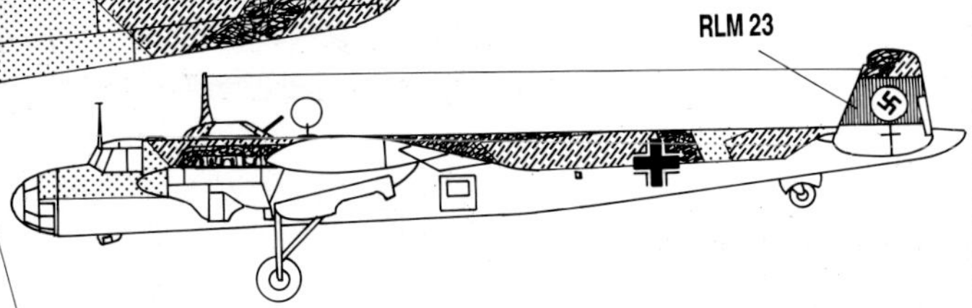

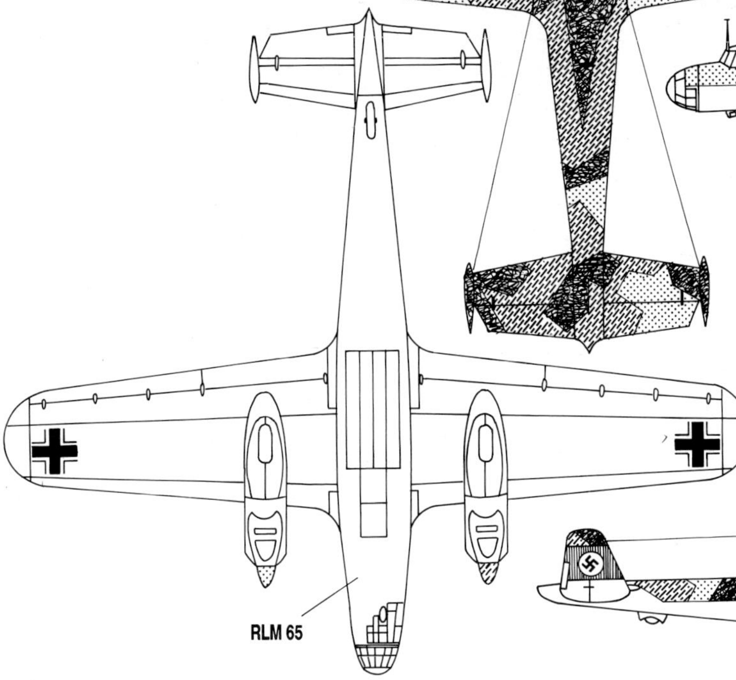

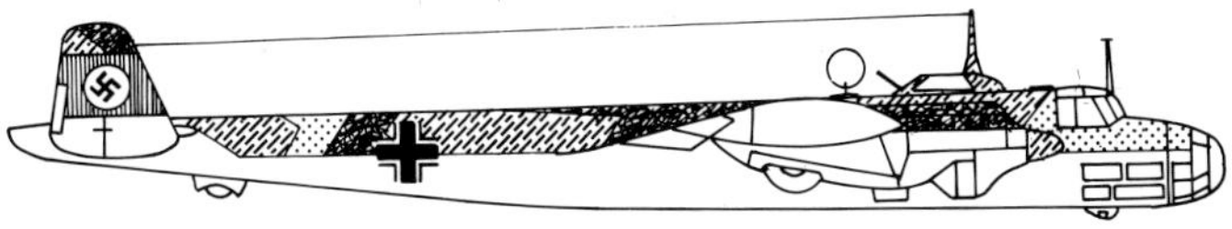

DORNIER 17 E–1

Standard A camouflage scheme of 1936 for the Dornier 17E/F/P bomber. The colours used: upper surfaces RLM 61 Dunkelbraun dark brown, RLM 62 Grün – green, and RLM 63 Grüngrau – light grey-green; under surfaces RLM 65 Hellblau – light blue. The camouflage colours could be exchanged but within the same division lines. Another scheme existed, which was a mirror image of the A2a scheme. Black swastika in white disc was applied on a red band on the vertical tail. The Balkenkreuz in proportions of 1936. Inner sides of vertical tails in RLM 61. Propeller blades RLM 63.

Standard A2a camouflage scheme of 1936 for the Junkers 86A/D bomber. The colours used: upper surfaces RLM 61 Dunkelbraun – dark brown, RLM 62 Grün – green, and RLM 63 Grüngrau – light grey-green; under surfaces RLM 65 Hellblau – light blue. The camouflage colours could be exchanged but within the same division lines. Another scheme existed, which was a mirror image of the A scheme. Black swastika in white disc was applied on a red band on the vertical tail. The Balkenkreuz in proportions of 1936. Inner sides of vertical tails in RLM 61, outer sides in RLM 62.

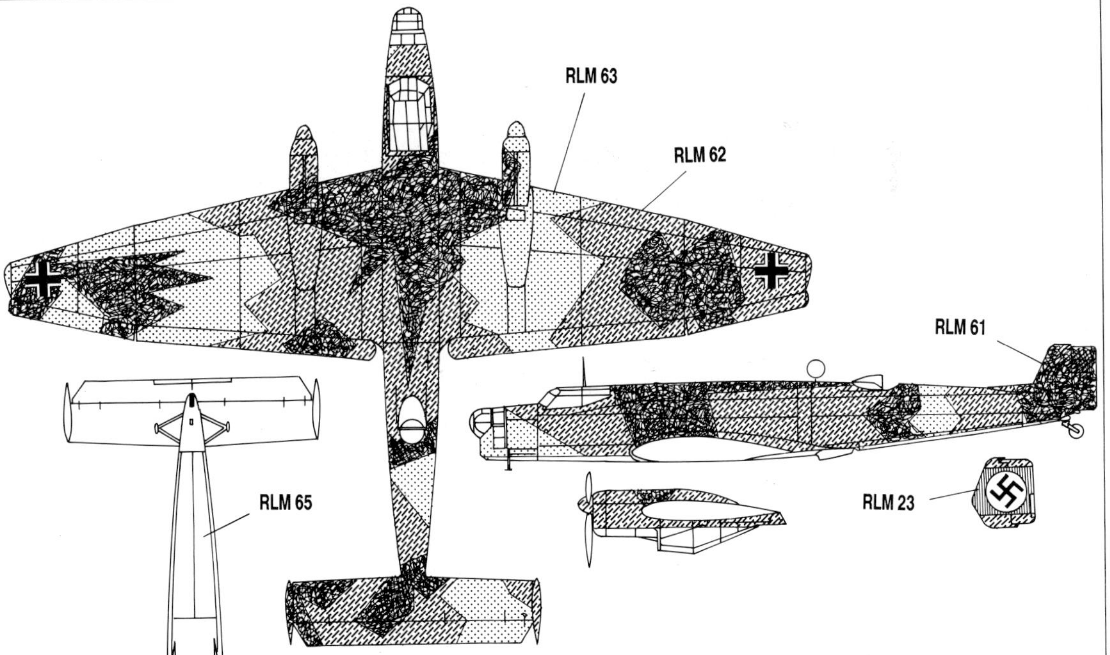

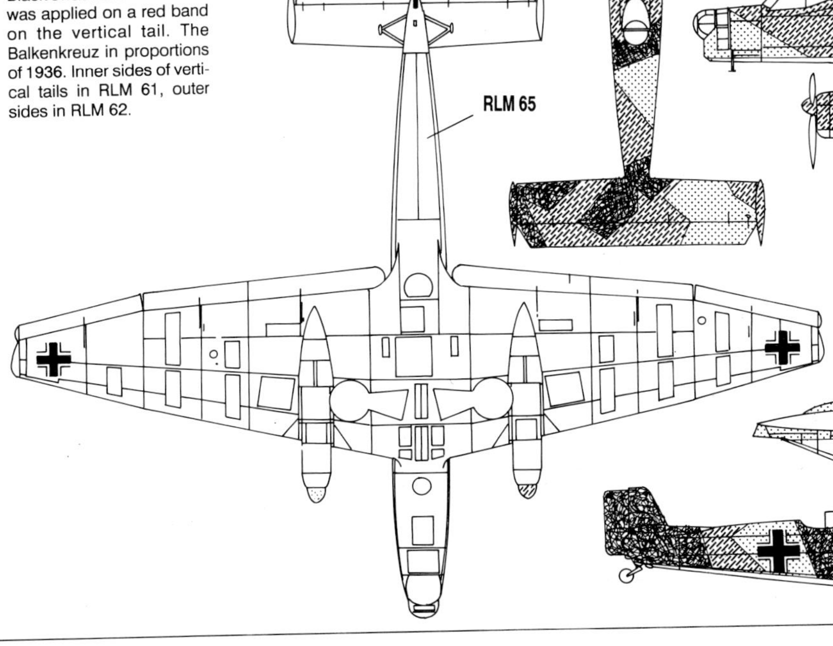

JUNKERS 86 A–1

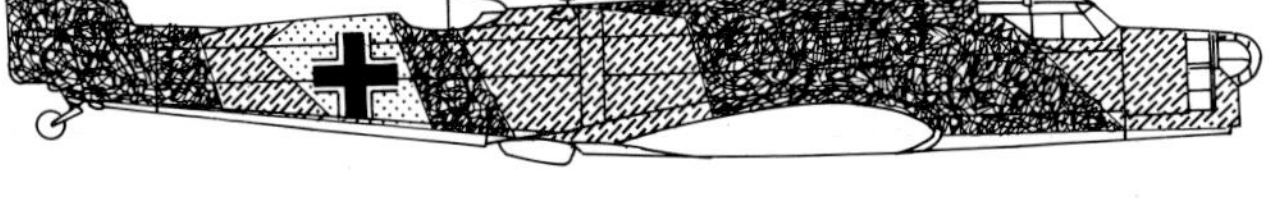

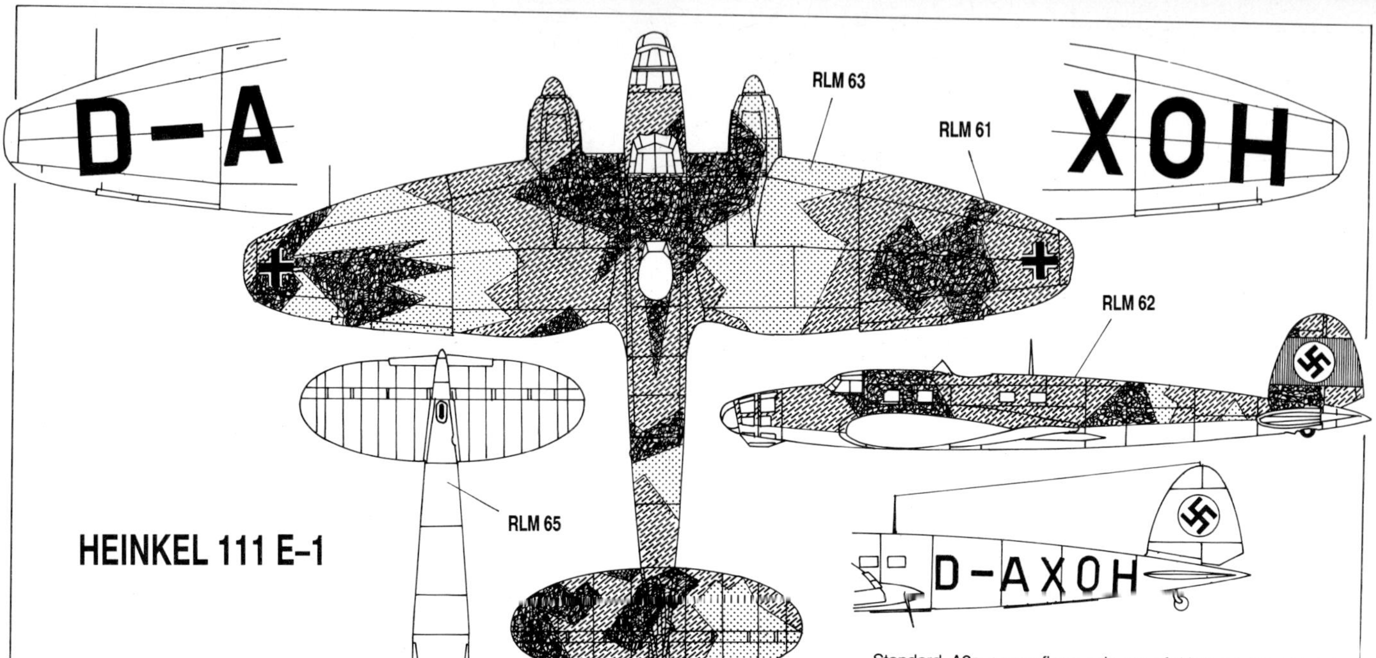

HEINKEL 111 E-1

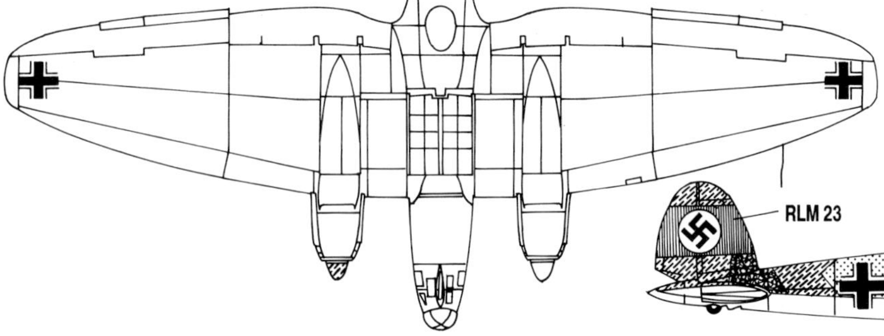

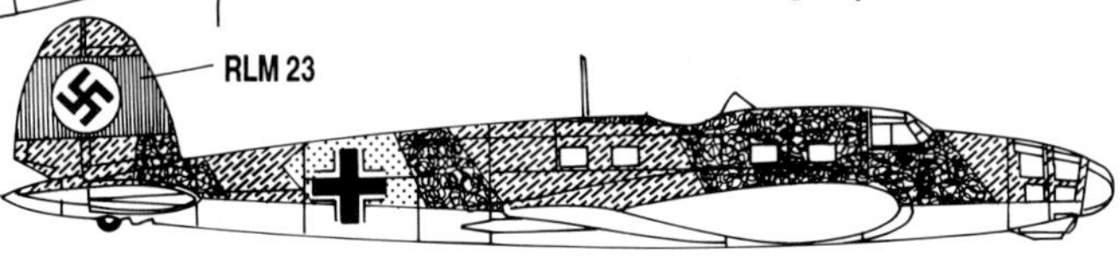

RLM 63

RLM 61

RLM 62

RLM 65

RLM 23

D-A XOH

D-AXOH

Standard A2a camouflage scheme of 1936 for the Heinkel 111B/D/E bomber. The colours used: upper surfaces RLM 61 Dunkelbraun dark brown, RLM 62 Grün – green, and RLM 63 Grüngrau – light grey-green; under surfaces RLM 65 Hellblau light blue. The camouflage colours could be exchanged but within the same division lines. Another scheme existed, which was a mirror image of the A2a scheme. Black swastika in white disc was applied on a red band on the vertical tail. The Balkenkreuz in proportions of 1936. Since 1933 the civil codes, for example, D–AXOH, in semi–glossy black.

HEINKEL 111 H-2

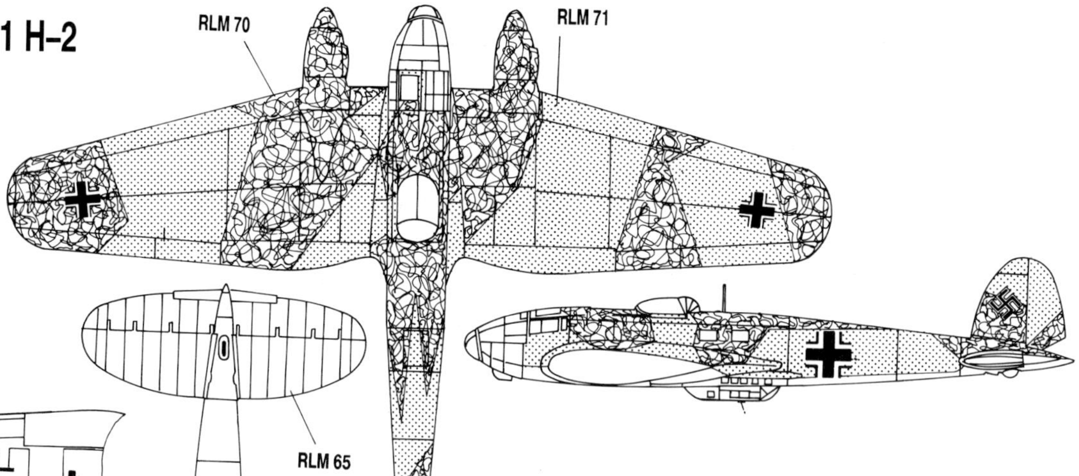

RLM 70

RLM 71

RLM 65

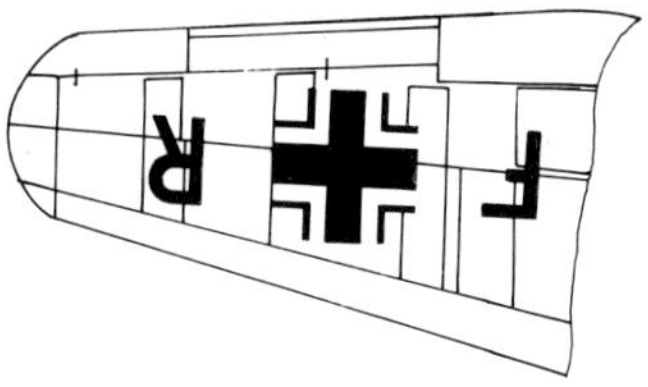

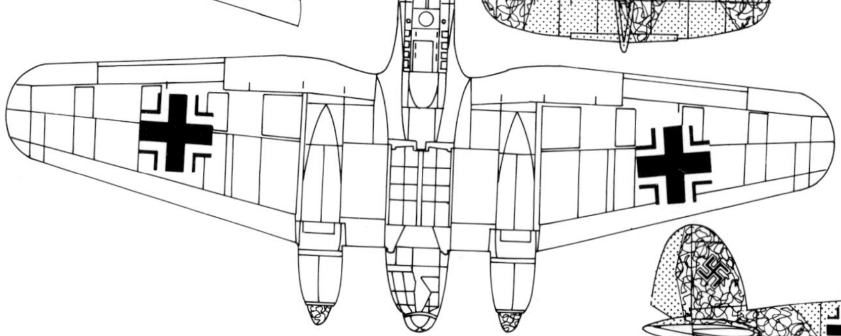

F R

Standard camouflage scheme for the Heinkel 111P/H bomber. The colours used: upper surfaces RLM 70 Schwarzgrün – black-green, and RLM 71 Dunkelgrün dark green; under surfaces RLM 65 Hellblau – light blue. The Balkenkreuz in proportions of 1936 (upper wing surface 100 cm x 100 cm) and of 1940 (under wing surface 200 cm x 200 cm, and fuselage 180 cm x 180 cm, later 140 cm x 140 cm). Hakenkreuz (swastika) 71 cm x 71 cm, later 65 cm x 65 cm. Propeller blades RLM 70.

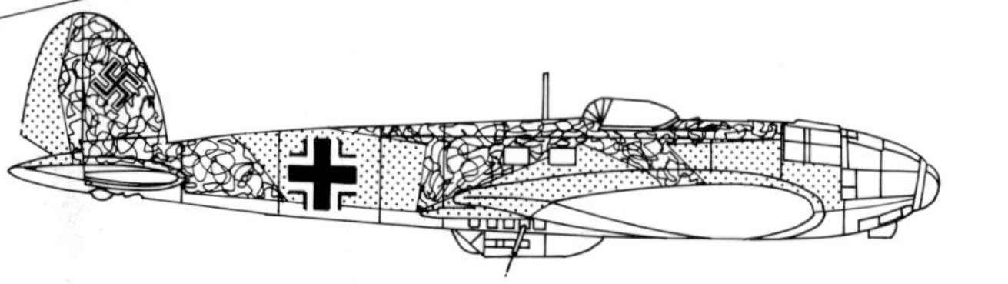

JUNKERS 88 A–4

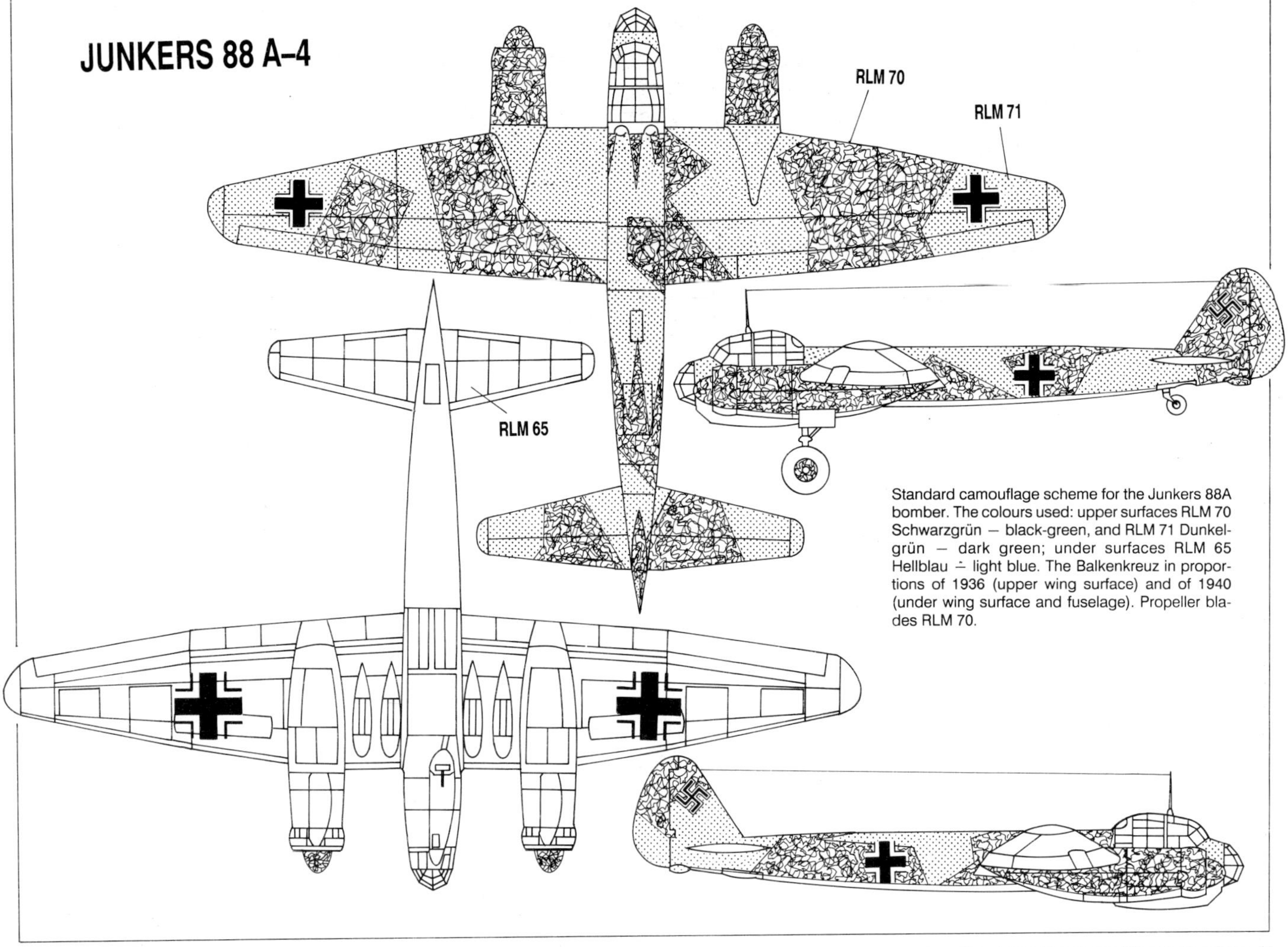

RLM 70

RLM 71

RLM 65

Standard camouflage scheme for the Junkers 88A bomber. The colours used: upper surfaces RLM 70 Schwarzgrün – black-green, and RLM 71 Dunkelgrün – dark green; under surfaces RLM 65 Hellblau – light blue. The Balkenkreuz in proportions of 1936 (upper wing surface) and of 1940 (under wing surface and fuselage). Propeller blades RLM 70.

JUNKERS 87 B–2

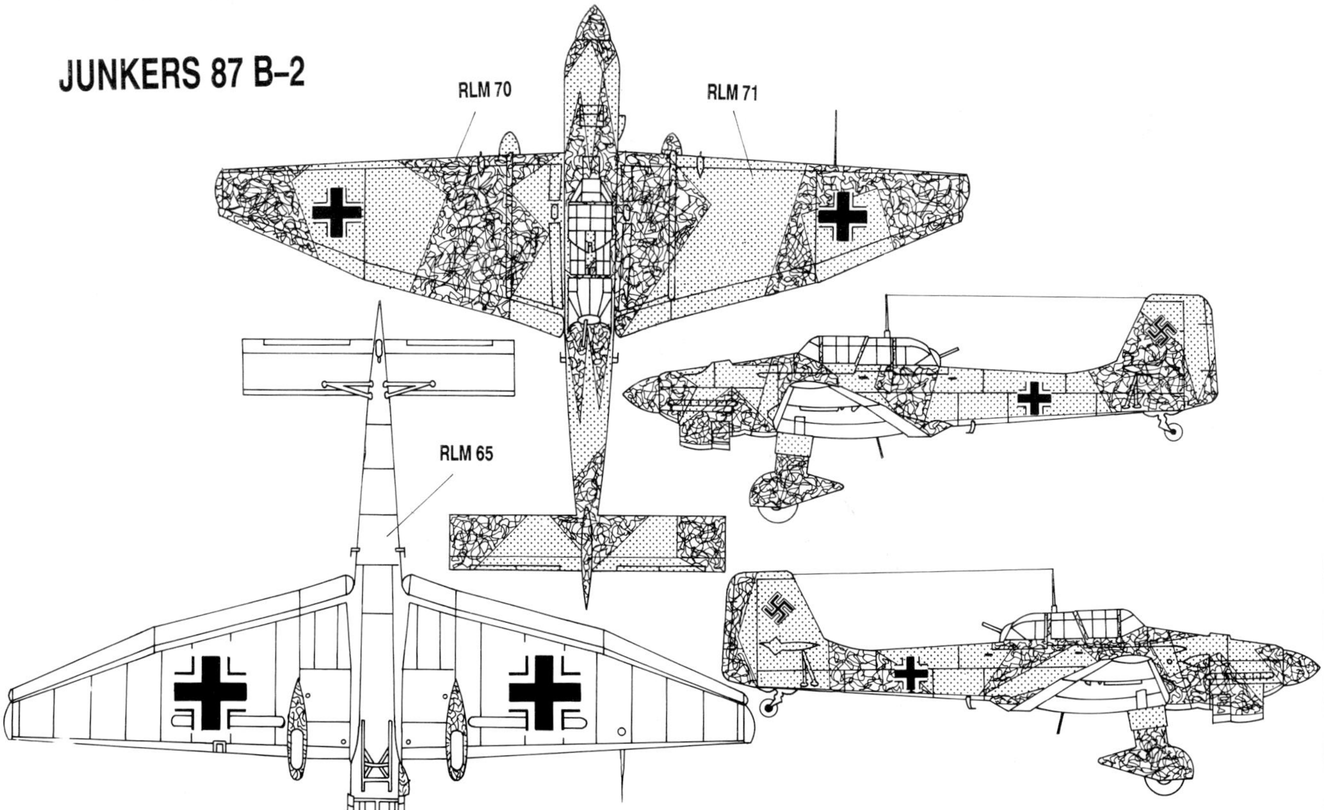

RLM 70

RLM 71

RLM 65

Standard camouflage scheme for the Junkers 87B/R Stuka dive bomber. The colours used: upper surfaces RLM 70 Schwarzgrün – black-green, and RLM 71 Dunkelgrün – dark green; under surfaces RLM 65 Hellblau – light blue. The Balkenkreuz in proportions of 1936 (upper wing surface) and of 1940 (under wing surface and fuselage). Propeller blades RLM 70.

FOCKE-WULF 189 A–1

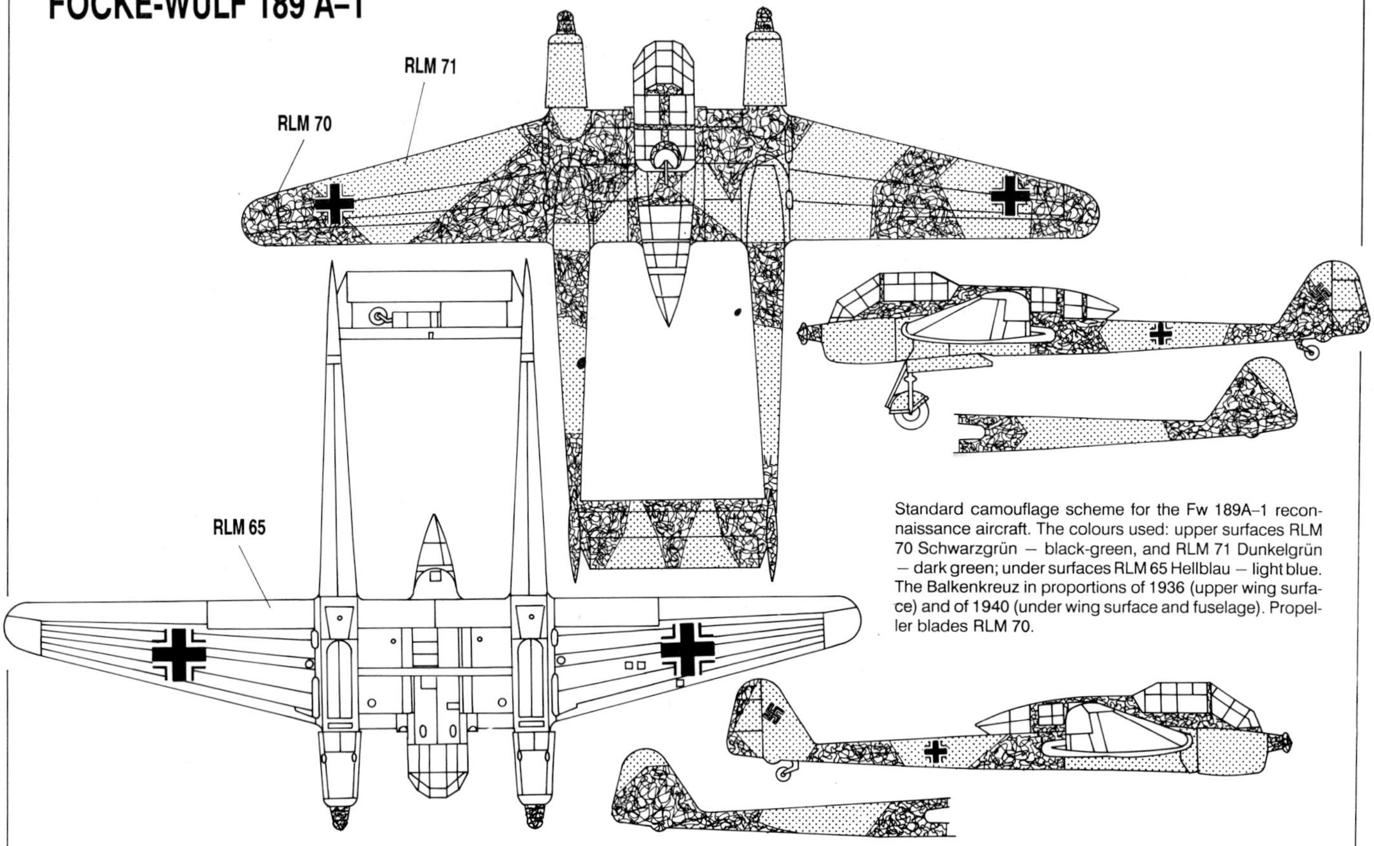

RLM 71

RLM 70

RLM 65

Standard camouflage scheme for the Fw 189A–1 reconnaissance aircraft. The colours used: upper surfaces RLM 70 Schwarzgrün – black-green, and RLM 71 Dunkelgrün – dark green; under surfaces RLM 65 Hellblau – light blue. The Balkenkreuz in proportions of 1936 (upper wing surface) and of 1940 (under wing surface and fuselage). Propeller blades RLM 70.

RLM 70

JUNKERS 52/3m

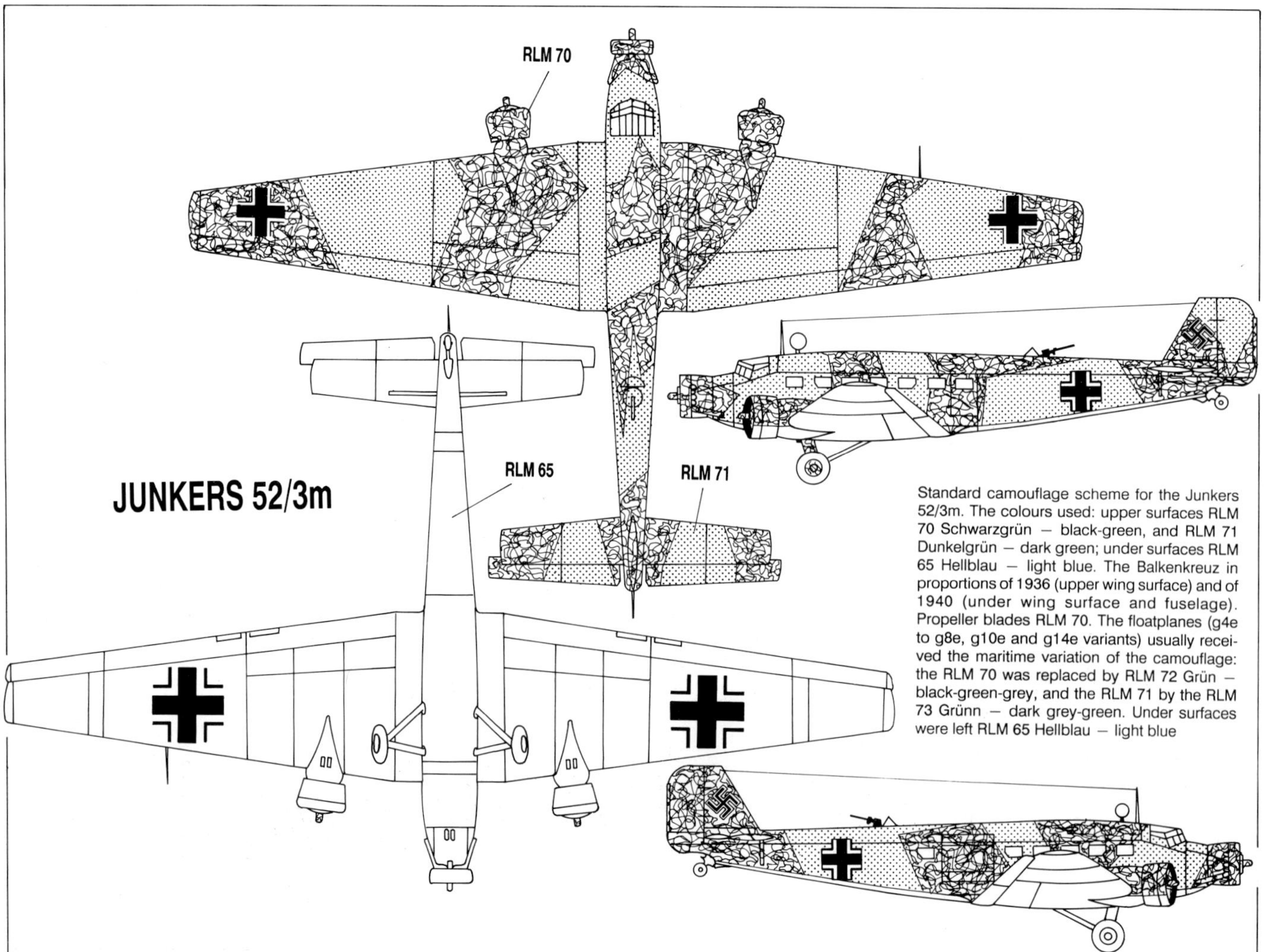

RLM 65

RLM 71

Standard camouflage scheme for the Junkers 52/3m. The colours used: upper surfaces RLM 70 Schwarzgrün – black-green, and RLM 71 Dunkelgrün – dark green; under surfaces RLM 65 Hellblau – light blue. The Balkenkreuz in proportions of 1936 (upper wing surface) and of 1940 (under wing surface and fuselage). Propeller blades RLM 70. The floatplanes (g4e to g8e, g10e and g14e variants) usually received the maritime variation of the camouflage: the RLM 70 was replaced by RLM 72 Grün – black-green-grey, and the RLM 71 by the RLM 73 Grünn – dark grey-green. Under surfaces were left RLM 65 Hellblau – light blue

HENSCHEL 126 A–1

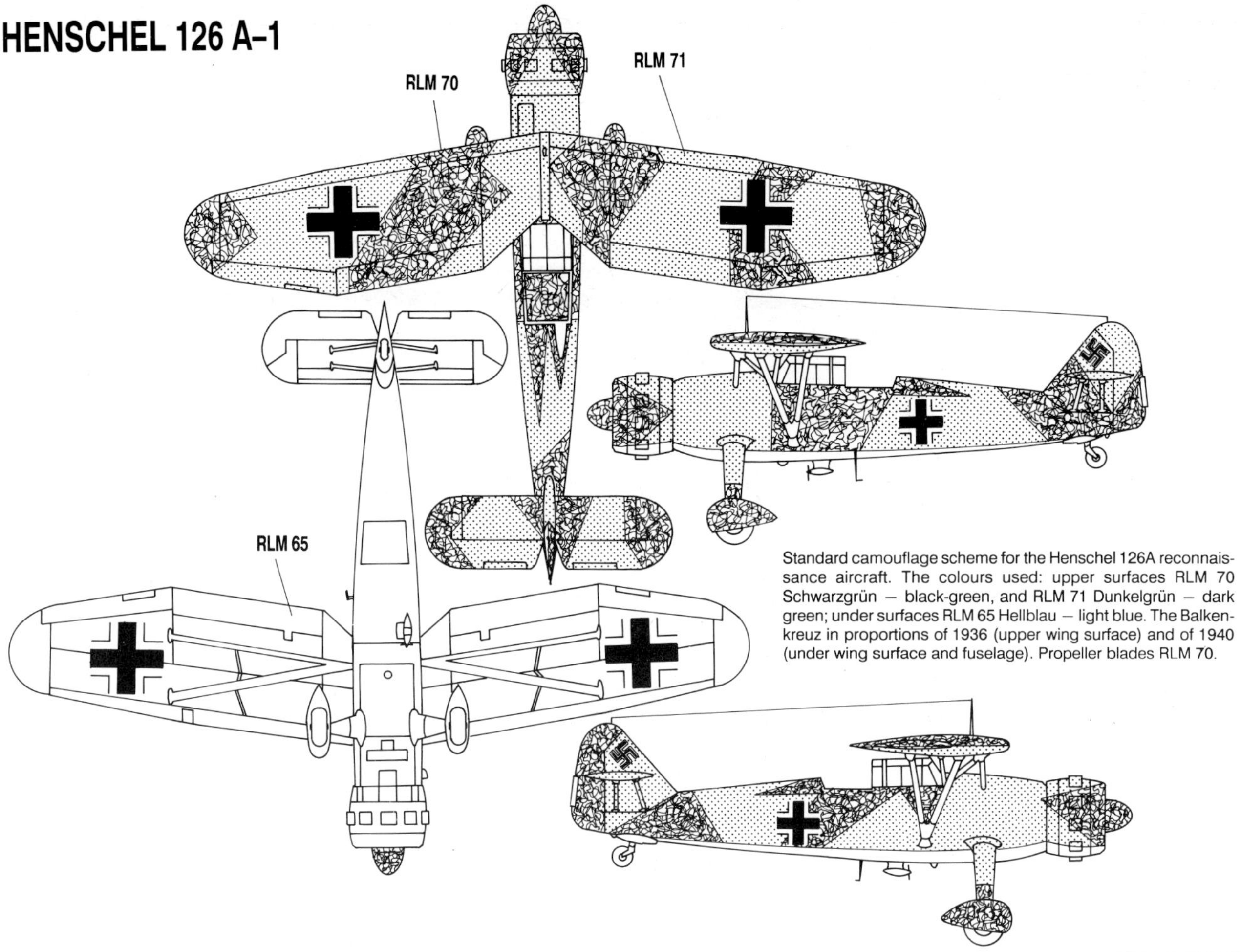

RLM 70

RLM 71

RLM 65

Standard camouflage scheme for the Henschel 126A reconnaissance aircraft. The colours used: upper surfaces RLM 70 Schwarzgrün – black-green, and RLM 71 Dunkelgrün – dark green; under surfaces RLM 65 Hellblau – light blue. The Balkenkreuz in proportions of 1936 (upper wing surface) and of 1940 (under wing surface and fuselage). Propeller blades RLM 70.

FIESELER 156 C–2

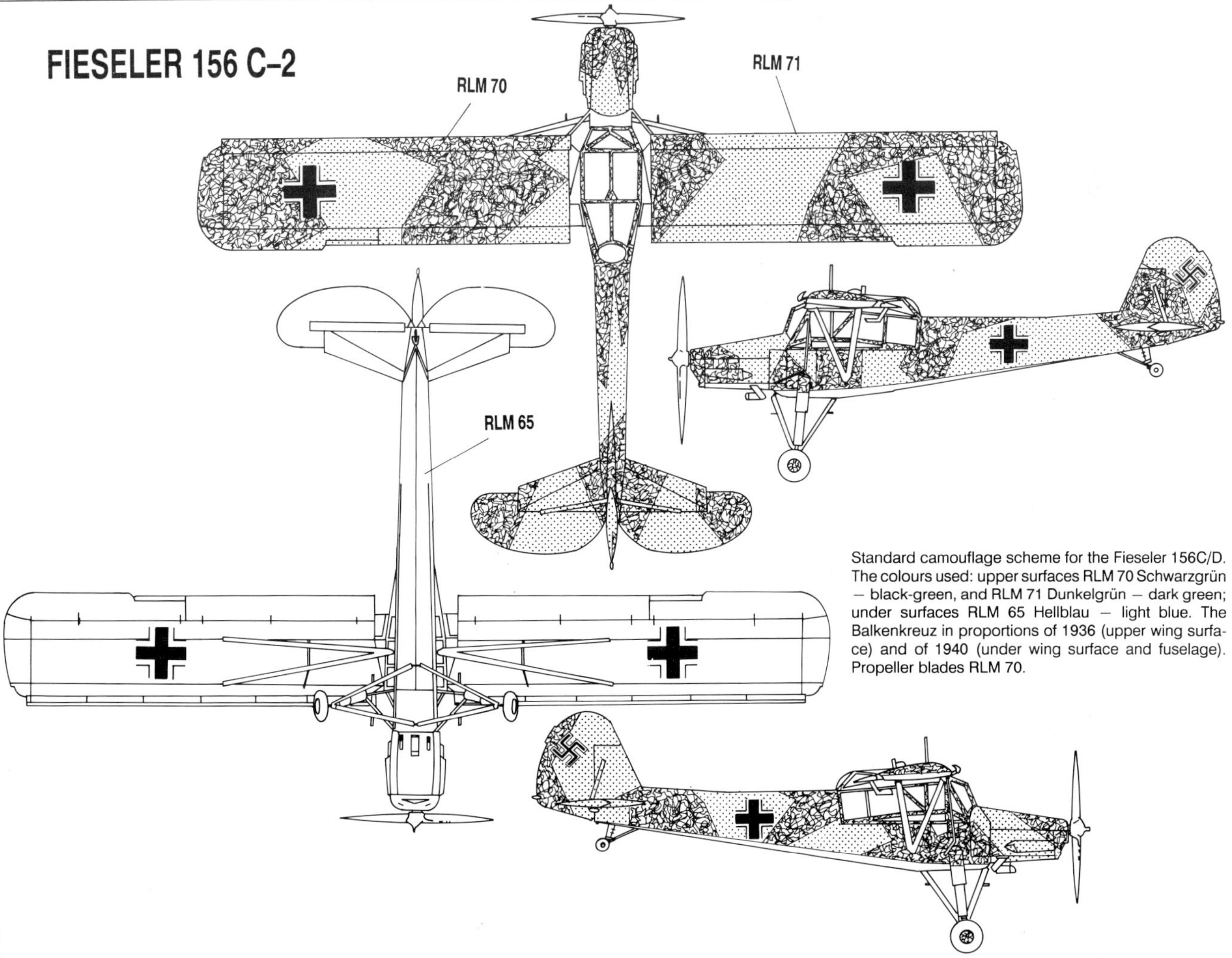

RLM 70

RLM 71

RLM 65

Standard camouflage scheme for the Fieseler 156C/D. The colours used: upper surfaces RLM 70 Schwarzgrün – black-green, and RLM 71 Dunkelgrün – dark green; under surfaces RLM 65 Hellblau – light blue. The Balkenkreuz in proportions of 1936 (upper wing surface) and of 1940 (under wing surface and fuselage). Propeller blades RLM 70.

Messerschmitt Bf 110 C

Standard camouflage scheme for the Messerschmitt Bf 110 B/C destroyer (heavy fighter) aircraft. The colours used: upper surfaces RLM 70 Schwarzgrün – black-green, and RLM 71 Dunkelgrün – dark green; under surfaces RLM 65 Hellblau – light blue. The Balkenkreuz in proportions of 1936 (upper wing surface) and of 1940 (under wing surface and fuselage). Propeller blades RLM 70.

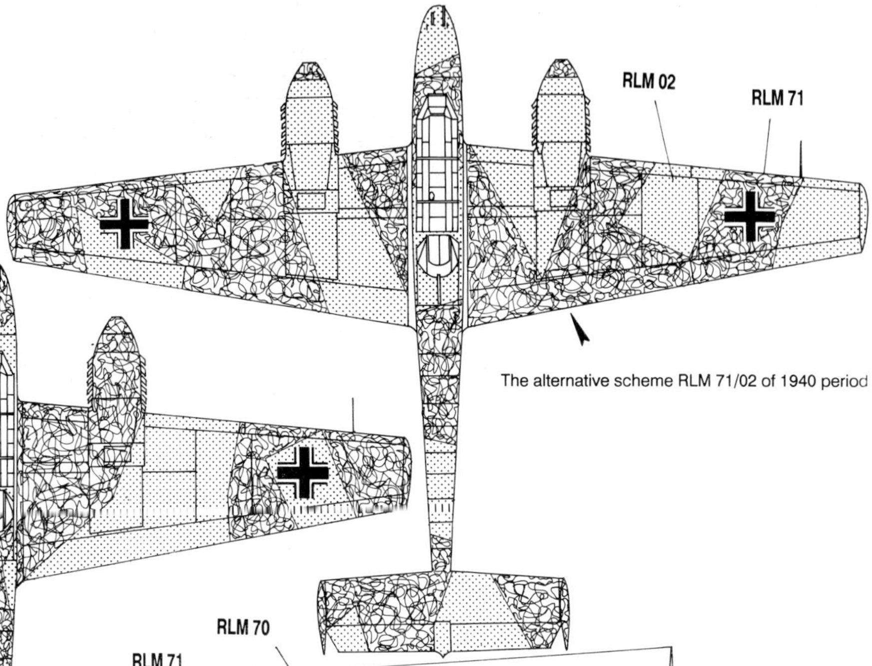

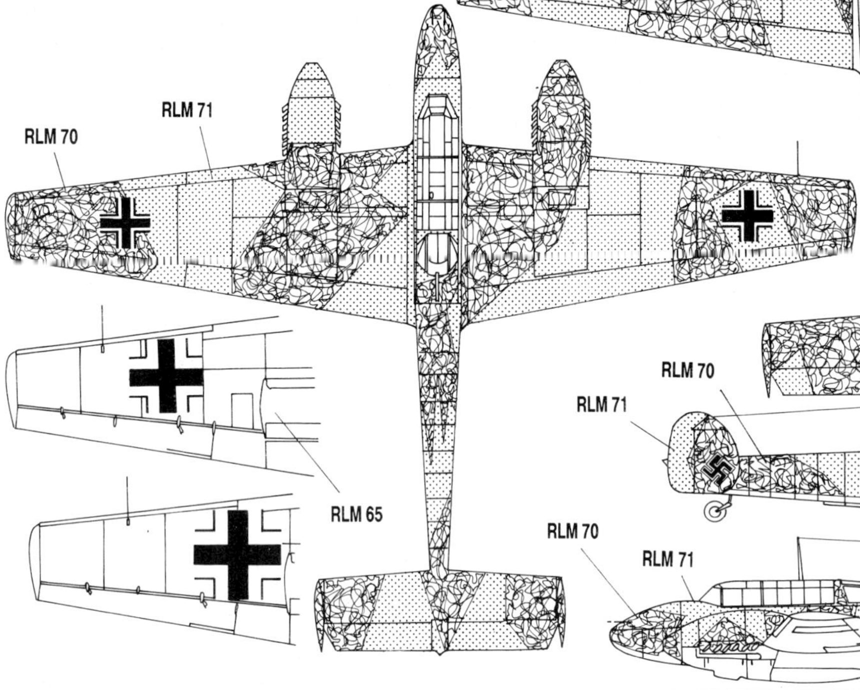

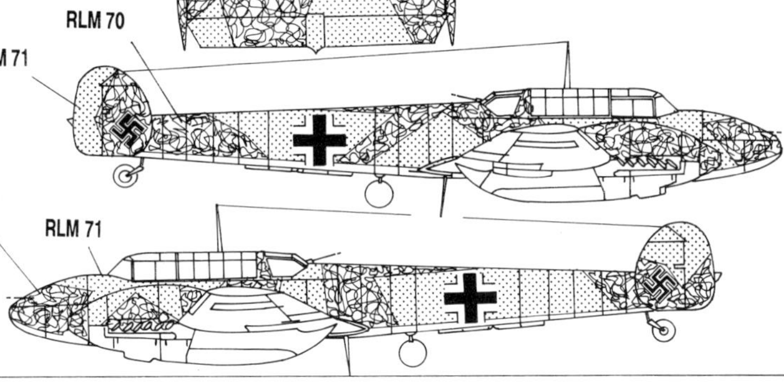

Messerschmitt Bf 108 B-1

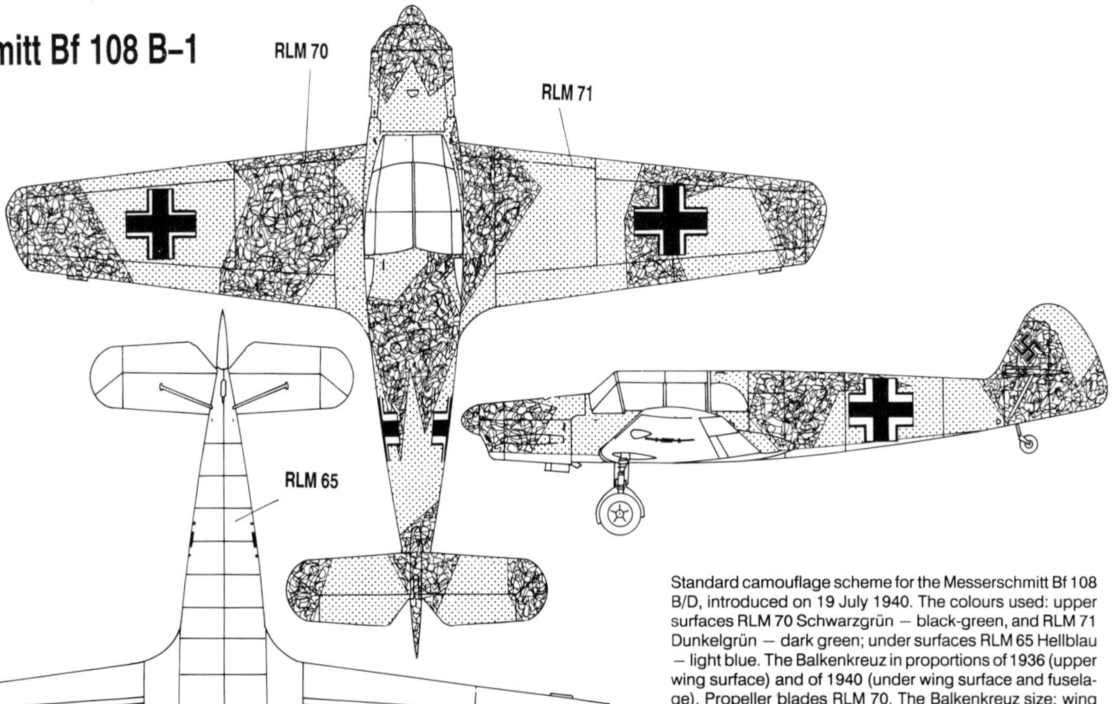

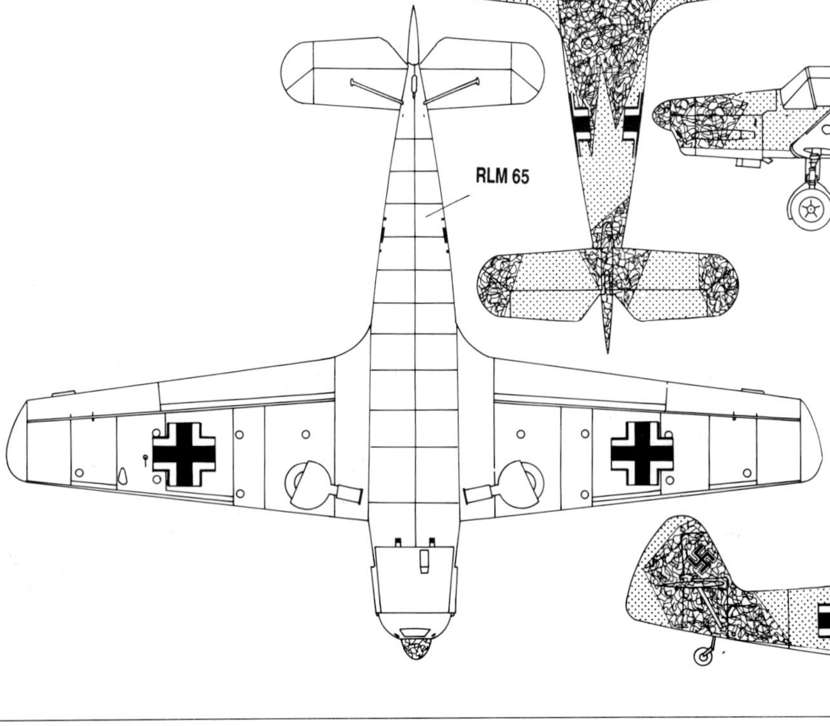

Standard camouflage scheme for the Messerschmitt Bf 108 B/D, introduced on 19 July 1940. The colours used: upper surfaces RLM 70 Schwarzgrün – black-green, and RLM 71 Dunkelgrün – dark green; under surfaces RLM 65 Hellblau – light blue. The Balkenkreuz in proportions of 1936 (upper wing surface) and of 1940 (under wing surface and fuselage). Propeller blades RLM 70. The Balkenkreuz size: wing upper surface – 90 cm x 90 cm, wing under surface – 80 cm x 80 cm, fuselage – 80 cm x 80 cm, later 75 cm x 75 cm. Hakenkreuz (swastika) 30 cm x 30 cm.

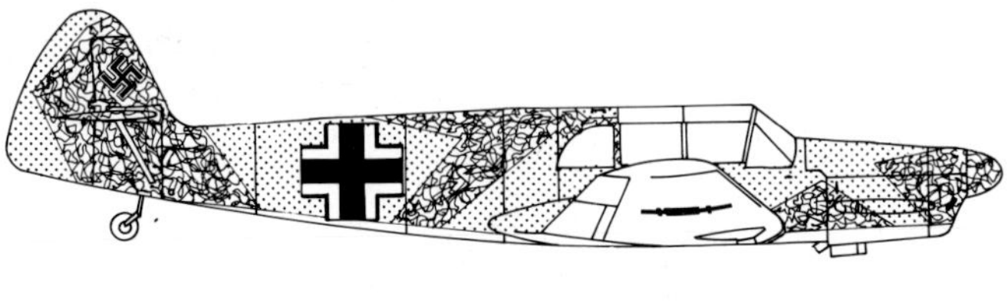

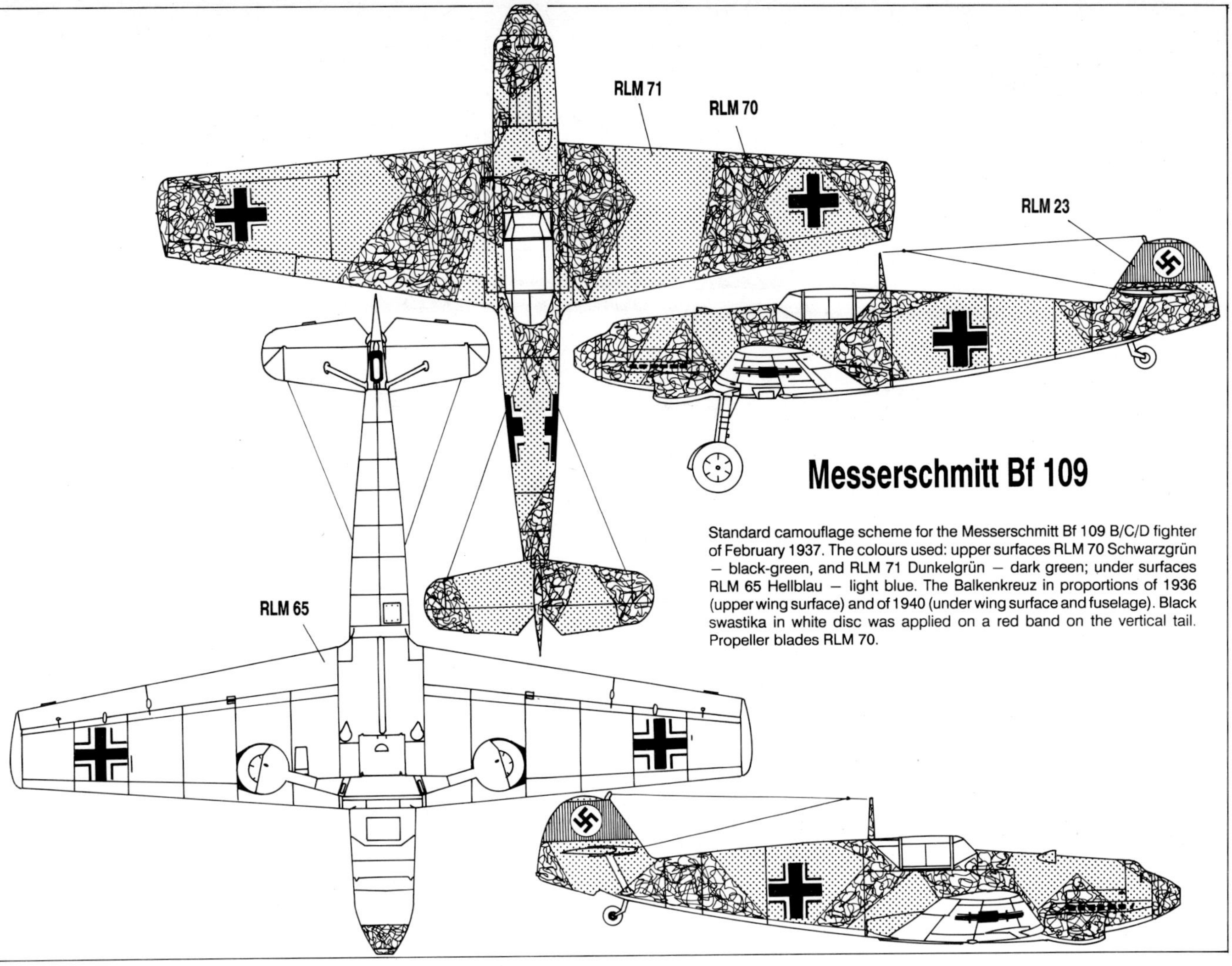

RLM 71

RLM 70

RLM 23

RLM 65

Messerschmitt Bf 109

Standard camouflage scheme for the Messerschmitt Bf 109 B/C/D fighter of February 1937. The colours used: upper surfaces RLM 70 Schwarzgrün – black-green, and RLM 71 Dunkelgrün – dark green; under surfaces RLM 65 Hellblau – light blue. The Balkenkreuz in proportions of 1936 (upper wing surface) and of 1940 (under wing surface and fuselage). Black swastika in white disc was applied on a red band on the vertical tail. Propeller blades RLM 70.

Messerschmitt Bf 109 E

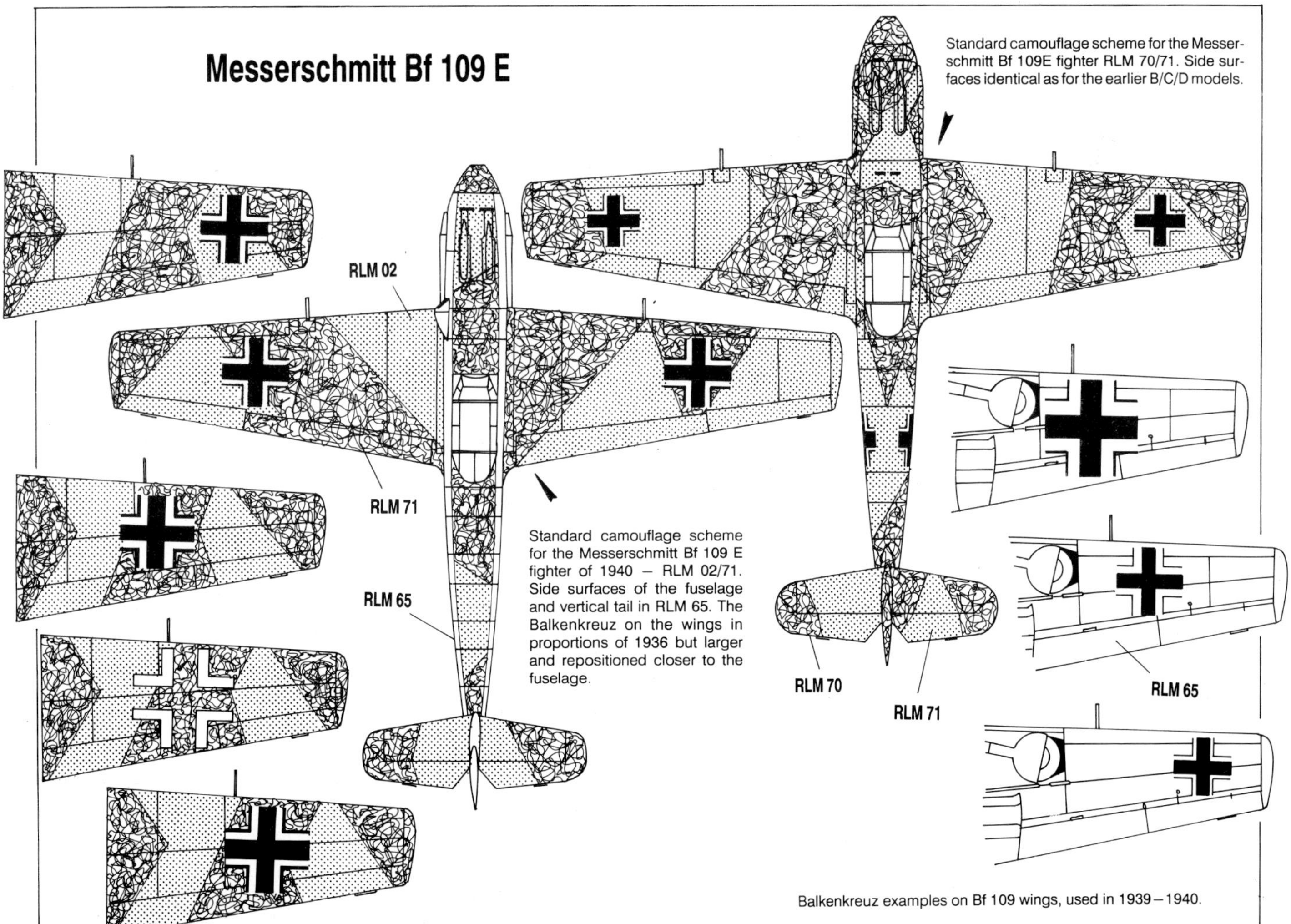

Standard camouflage scheme for the Messerschmitt Bf 109E fighter RLM 70/71. Side surfaces identical as for the earlier B/C/D models.

RLM 02

RLM 71

RLM 65

Standard camouflage scheme for the Messerschmitt Bf 109 E fighter of 1940 – RLM 02/71. Side surfaces of the fuselage and vertical tail in RLM 65. The Balkenkreuz on the wings in proportions of 1936 but larger and repositioned closer to the fuselage.

RLM 70

RLM 71

RLM 65

Balkenkreuz examples on Bf 109 wings, used in 1939–1940.

DORNIER 18 G-1

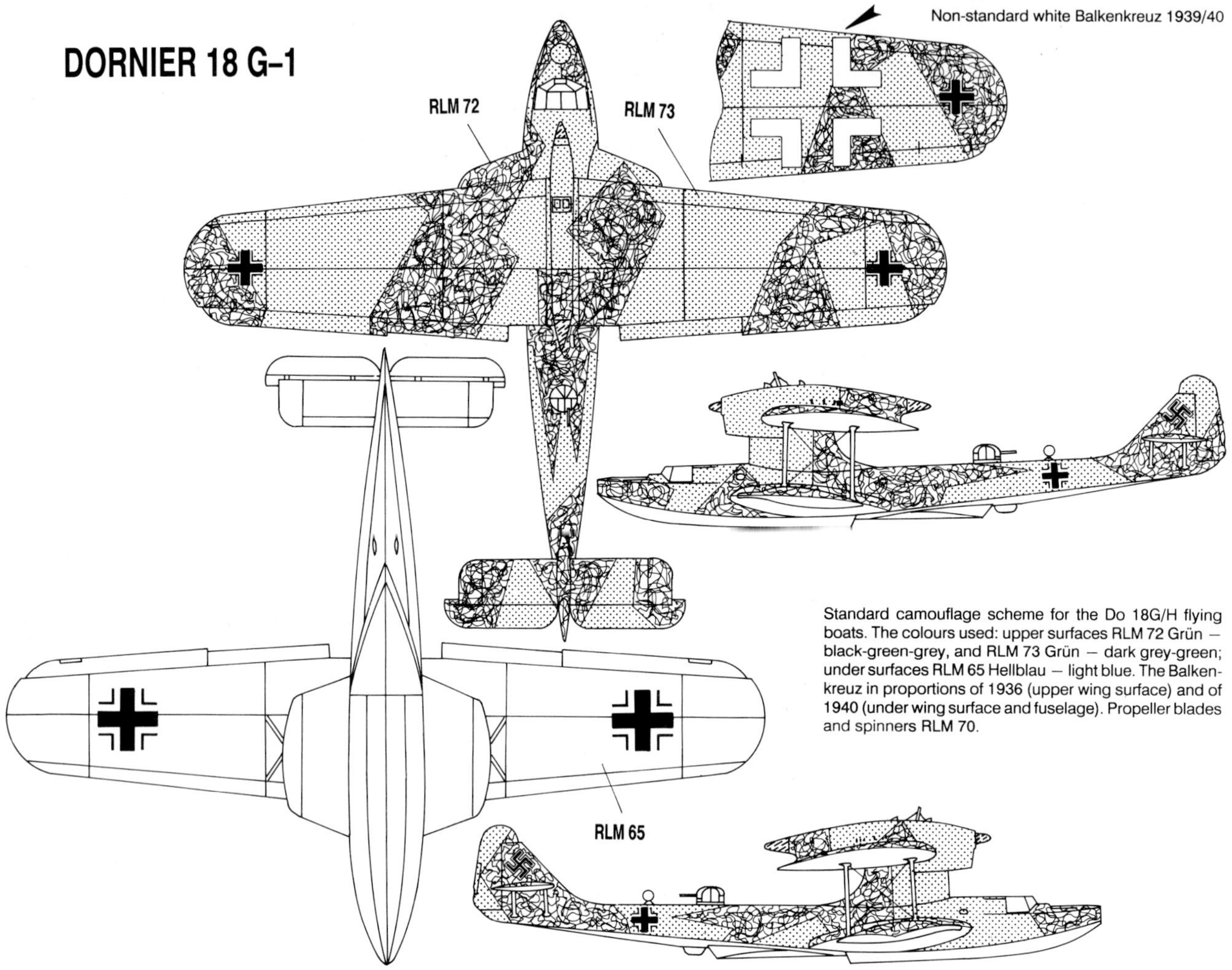

Standard camouflage scheme for the Do 18G/H flying boats. The colours used: upper surfaces RLM 72 Grün – black-green-grey, and RLM 73 Grün – dark grey-green; under surfaces RLM 65 Hellblau – light blue. The Balkenkreuz in proportions of 1936 (upper wing surface) and of 1940 (under wing surface and fuselage). Propeller blades and spinners RLM 70.

DORNIER 24 T-1

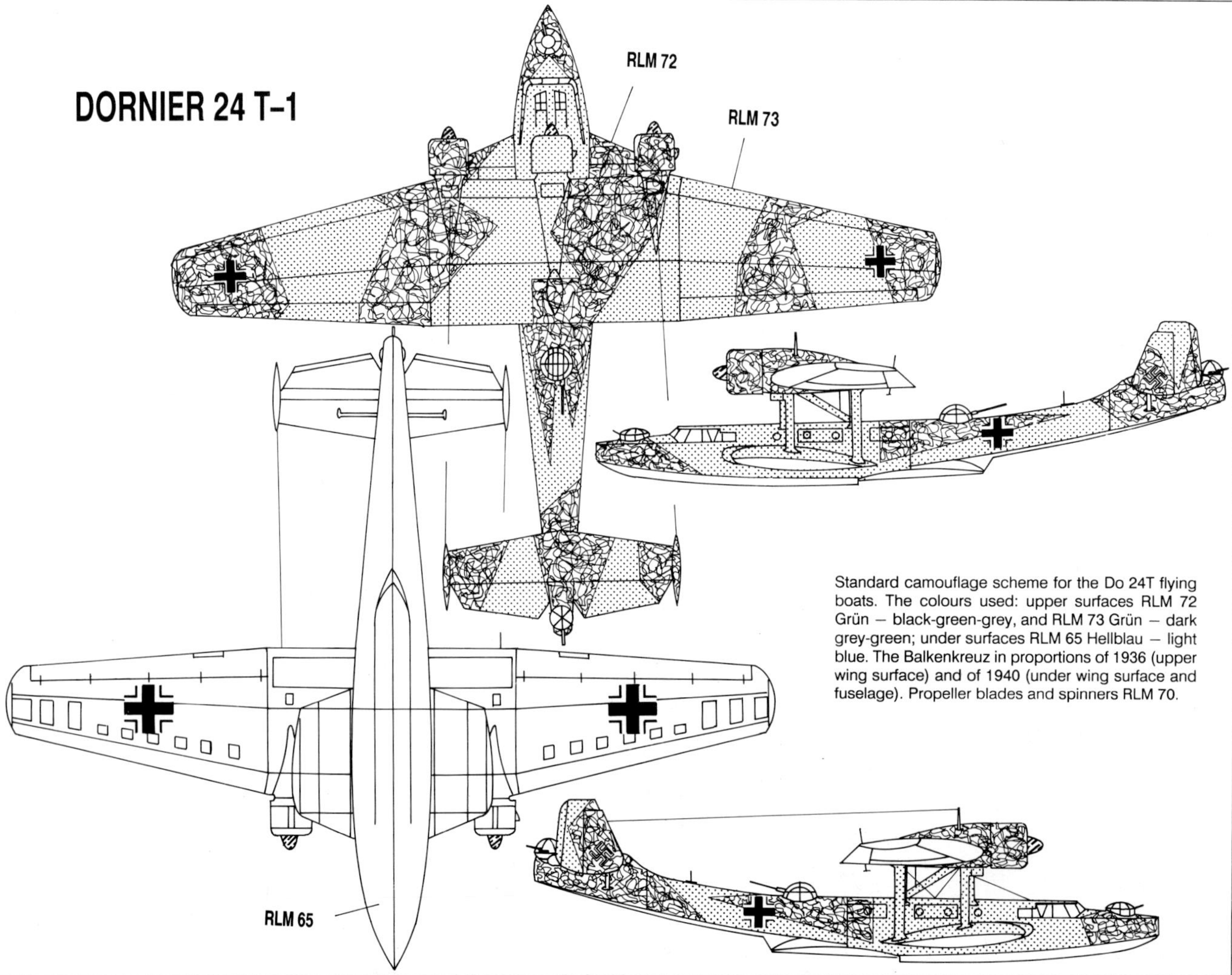

Standard camouflage scheme for the Do 24T flying boats. The colours used: upper surfaces RLM 72 Grün – black-green-grey, and RLM 73 Grün – dark grey-green; under surfaces RLM 65 Hellblau – light blue. The Balkenkreuz in proportions of 1936 (upper wing surface) and of 1940 (under wing surface and fuselage). Propeller blades and spinners RLM 70.

DORNIER 26 D–0

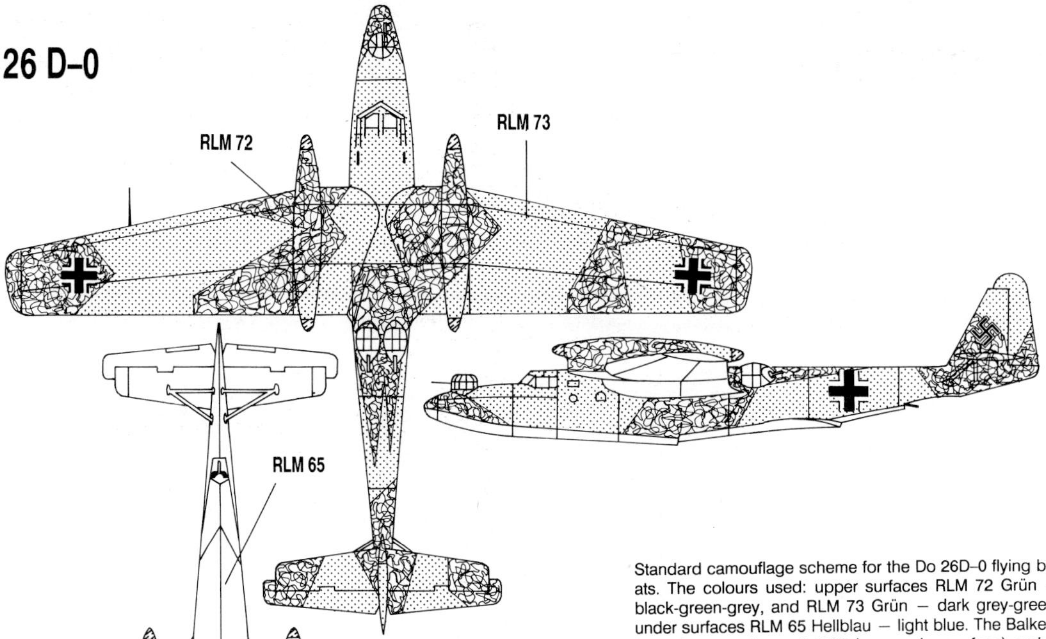

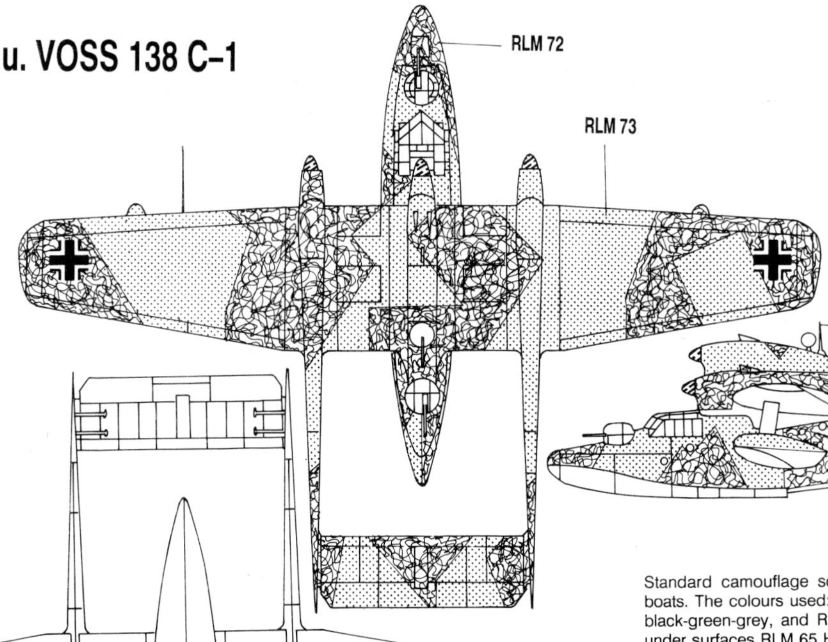

RLM 72

RLM 73

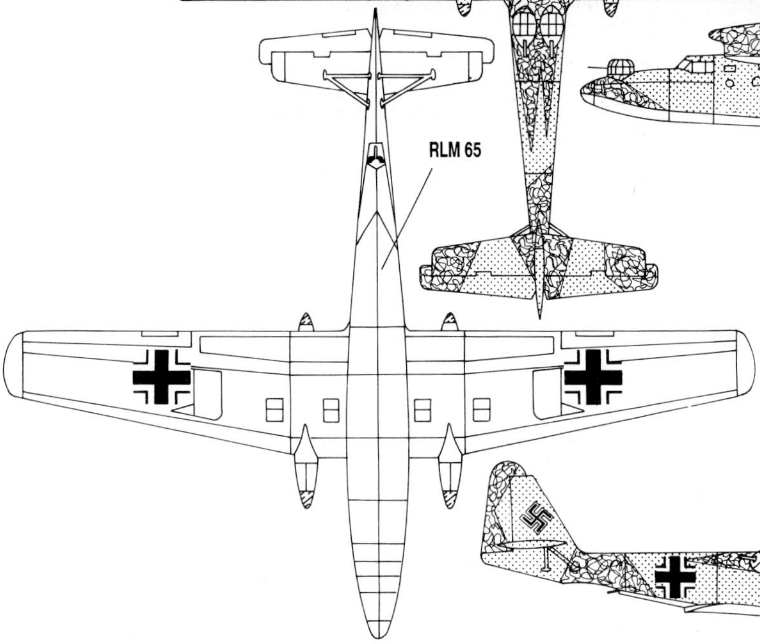

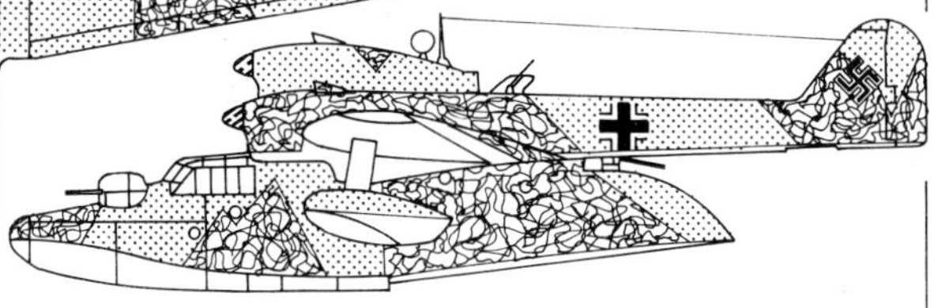

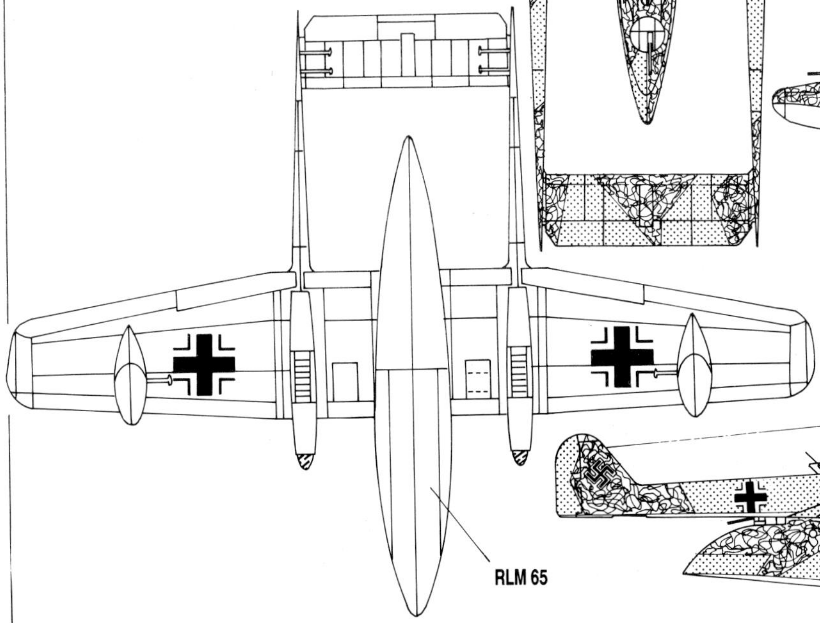

RLM 65

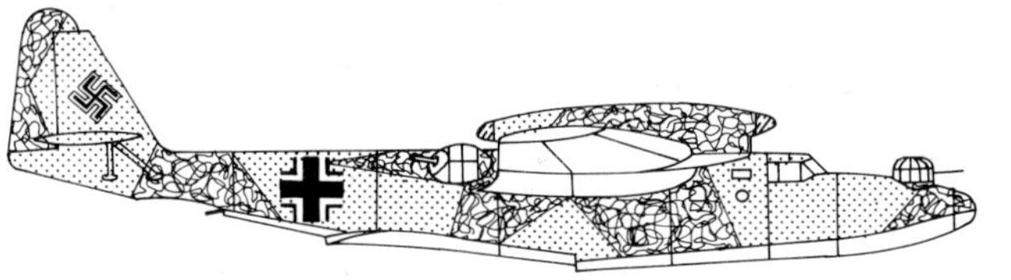

Standard camouflage scheme for the Do 26D–0 flying boats. The colours used: upper surfaces RLM 72 Grün – black-green-grey, and RLM 73 Grün – dark grey-green; under surfaces RLM 65 Hellblau – light blue. The Balkenkreuz in proportions of 1936 (upper wing surface) and of 1940 (under wing surface and fuselage). Propeller blades and spinners RLM 70.

BLOHM u. VOSS 138 C–1

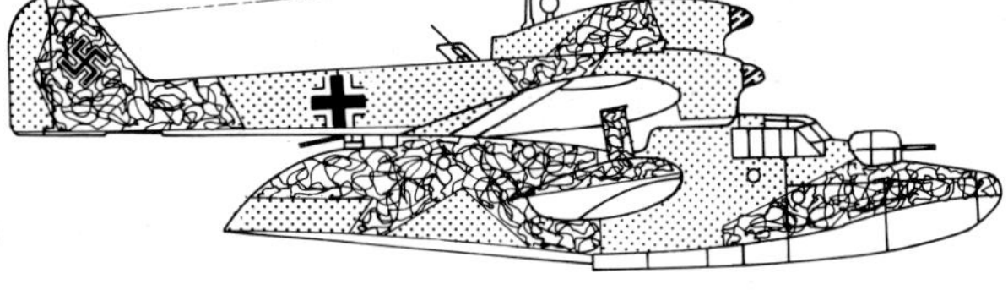

RLM 72

RLM 73

Standard camouflage scheme for the Bv 138B/C flying boats. The colours used: upper surfaces RLM 72 Grün – black-green-grey, and RLM 73 Grün – dark grey-green; under surfaces RLM 65 Hellblau – light blue. The Balkenkreuz in proportions of 1936 (upper wing surface) and of 1940 (under wing surface and fuselage). Propeller blades and spinners RLM 70.

RLM 65

A formation of He 51Cs of 1. J/88 Condor Legion, Spain, 1937. The aircraft in foreground, coded 2•64, was piloted by Staffelkäpitan Harro Harder. His personal emblem – white swastika – was painted on the fuselage black circle. In the shadow of the upper wing is – not well visible in this photo – the 1. flight emblem – Marabu. The aircraft carried non standard camouflage composed of RLM 61 spots painted on the upper and side RLM 63 areas.

(P. Jarrett via B. Ketley)

THE CONDOR LEGION.

During the civil war in Spain (1936–39) the Germans were engaged on the Nationalist side of Gen. Franco. At his request Germans established a unit called the Condor Legion, with over 30 types of aircraft on strenght. Among them were fighters, bombers, reconnaissance, cargo and utility aircraft. Those aircraft were generally finished in standard Luftwaffe camouflage but did not wear German national insignia. Aircraft such as the Messerschmitt Bf 109, Bf 108, Heinkel He 46, He 51, Arado Ar 68 wore the dominant scheme light grey-green (RLM 63) or grey (RLM 02) overall. From 1937, many of the Bf 109s had their undersides in RLM 65, with upper surfaces in light grey-green; in 1938 the fighter of lnt. Wolfgang Schellman – commander of 1./J 88, marked with code 651 was an example of such painting. Some Heinkel He 51s wore on their upper surfaces and fuselage sides the Luftwaffe camouflage of RLM 61/62/63 areas, with the undersides painted in standard blue (RLM 65). It was of interest to test the qualities of offensive and defensive camouflage.

The Heinkel He 51s did not carry any special markings, except for leut. Haro Harder, which wore a white swastika inside

The He 111 B–1 coded 25•17 of 1.K/88 with a very dirty (additional Painting?) fuselage. The plane have a RLM 63 camouflage.

(IDHYCA via R. Michulec)

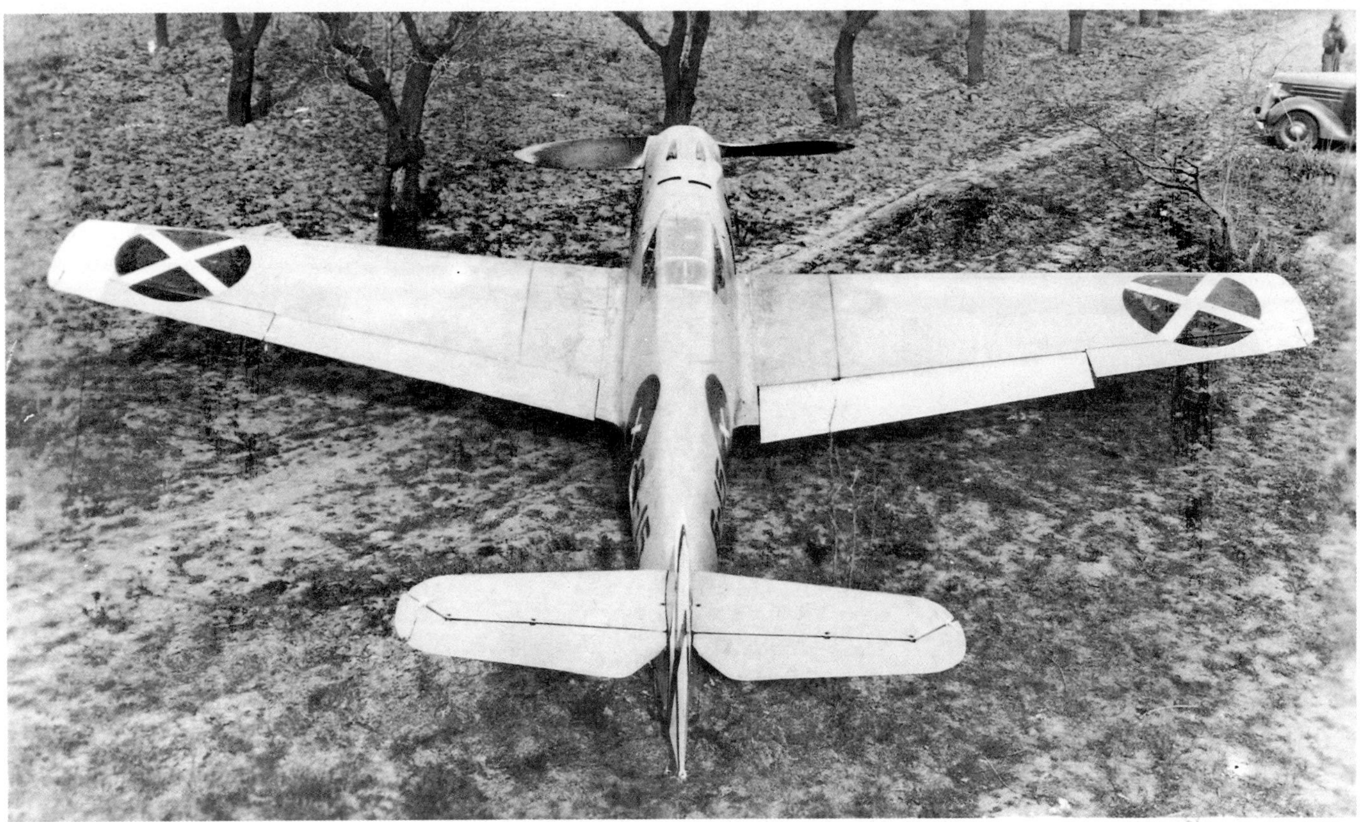

Fine view of a Messerschmitt Bf 109B–1 6●15 of 2./JGr 88 Condor Legion. Well visible positioning of black and white nationalist markings.
(P. Jarrett via B. Ketley)

Franco's air force insignia (a black disc). Initially He 51s did not carry personal insignia. Generally the first insignia painted on the Condor Legion aircraft was a green heart – "Grünherz" – individual emblem of leut Hannes Trautloft. The prototype Messerschmitt Bf 109 (V3 or V4) was also marked with this symbol.

At the beginning of 1937, on the aircraft of J./88 of Legion Condor insignia of this wing was emerged – big cylinder drawing.

For the first time victory symbols – white vertical bars about 100 mm high – were applied on the Messerschmitt Bf 109 B–2 (6●36) belonging to Harro Harder. On the vertical tail of his aircraft three victories were marked: 1. – Polikarpov I–15, 2. and

Another shot of the same aircraft, this time in profile. Light grey (RLM 63) aircraft sports white rudder and wingtips for identification. Black 6●15 on the fuselage is the military code; "6" for Bf 109, "15" means the fifteenth aircraft of the type.
(P. Jarrett via B. Ketley)

FUSELAGE EMBLEMS AND PERSONAL MARKINGS OF CONDOR LEGION AIRCRAFT

Fuselage emblem on He 51B No. 2•98 piloted by Kurt Strümpell

Fuselage emblem on He 51B 4th Staffel insignia

Fuselage emblem on He 51B No. 2•78 piloted by Adolf Galland

Fuselage emblem on He 51B No. 2•64 piloted by Harro Harder

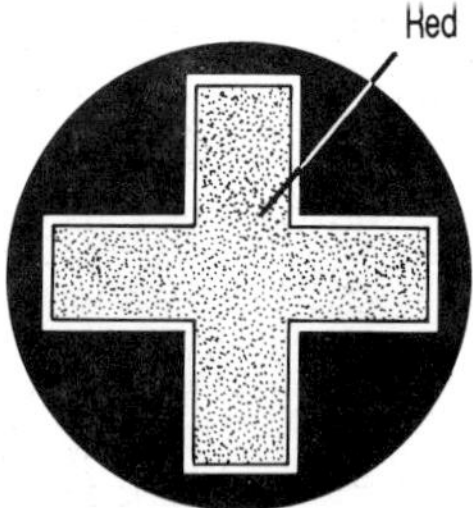

Fuselage emblem on He 51B No. 2•102 piloted by Dr Neumann

Fuselage emblem on He 51B No. 2•85 piloted by Dr Neumann

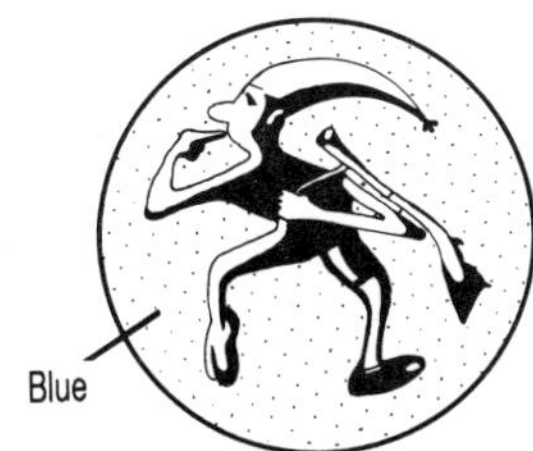

Personal marking on He 51B of 4th Staffel on November 1936

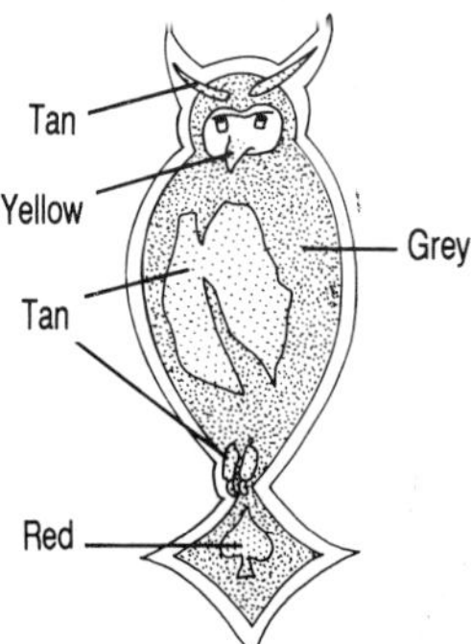

Squadron's emblem on Ar 68E No. 9•2 of Nachtjäger Staffel at La Cenia

Variation of 1st Staffel insignia on He 51B No. 2•64 piloted by Harro Harder

Variation of 1st Staffel insignia

Variation of 3rd Staffel insignia on He 51B No. 2•26

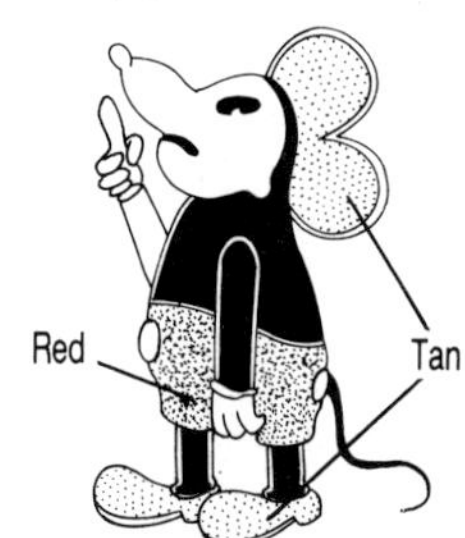

Fuselage insignia of 3rd Staffel

Fuselage insignia of 2nd Staffel

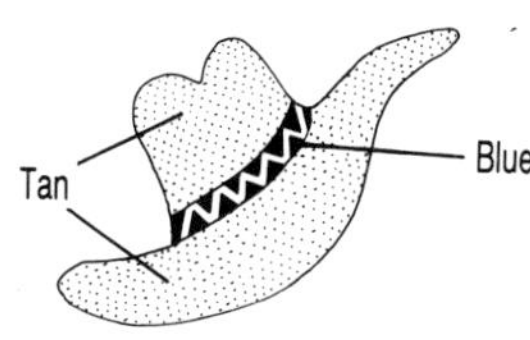

Personal fuselage marking on unknown He 51B

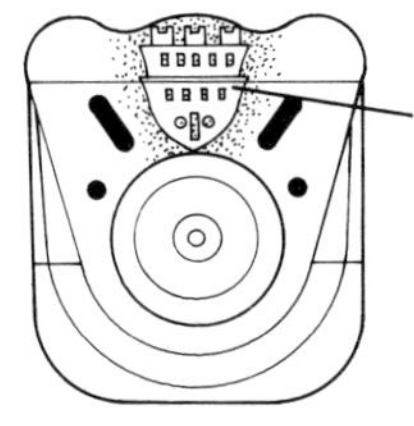

Cowl marking on He 51B No. 2•85 piloted by Dr. Neumann

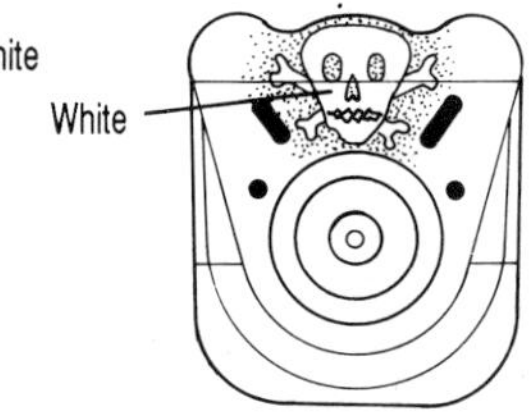

Cowl marking on unknown He 51B

3. – two SB–2. Similar symbols were among those used on the aircraft of leut. Erich Woitke (6•34). This practice was quickly adopted and all aircraft were marked this way. These symbols were painted only on the, left side of vertical tail and rarely on both sides – e.g. 5•51 of leut. Wolfgang Schellman, commander of 1./J88. Aircraft of other aces of the Condor Legion also had such markings – an example is the Messerschmitt Bf 109 D coded 6•79 of leut. Werner Mölders and caled "Luchs".

Interesting examples of pilot's individual markings that were painted inside the nationalist insignia of Franco's Air Force were the white letters „G" – used by Walter Grabmann, and „H" – used by Gothard Handrick. Sometimes the Condor Legion aircraft wore the individual insignia of the pilots, for example Bf 109 6•79 of Werner Mölders had a Micky Mouse and Bf 109 6•56 of Gothard Handrick had the Olympic insignia painted on the spinner (he was a winner of the pentathlon during the Berlin Olympic Games in 1936).

MILITARY CODES OF CONDOR LEGION AIRCRAFT USED DURING 1936–39 PERIOD	
CODE	TYPE
2	Heinkel He 51 "Cadenas"
6	Messerschmitt Bf 109 "Meser"
8	Heinkel He 112 V9, (later I-15 "Chato")
9	Arado Ar 68 E
11	Heinkel He 46 "Pava"
14	Heinkel He 70 "Rayo"
15	Heinkel He 45 "Pavo"
19	Henschel He 126 "Super Pava"
22	Junkers Ju 52 "Junker"
24	Henschel He 123 "Angelito"
25	Heinkel He 111
26	Junkers Ju 86 "Jumo"
27	Dornier Do 17 "Bacalao"
29	Junkers Ju 87 "Stupido"/"Stuka"
30	Klemm Kl 32, later RWD 13
33	Bücker Bü 131 "Jungmann"
35	Bücker Bü 133 „Jungmeister"
36	Arado Ar 66
38	Gotha Go 145
43	Junkers W 34
44	Messerschmitt Bf 108 "Tajfun"
46	Fieseler Fi 156 "Ciguena"
60	Heinkel He 60
64	Arado Ar 95
71	Heinkel He 59 "Zapatone"
72	Junkers Ju 52/3 m and W

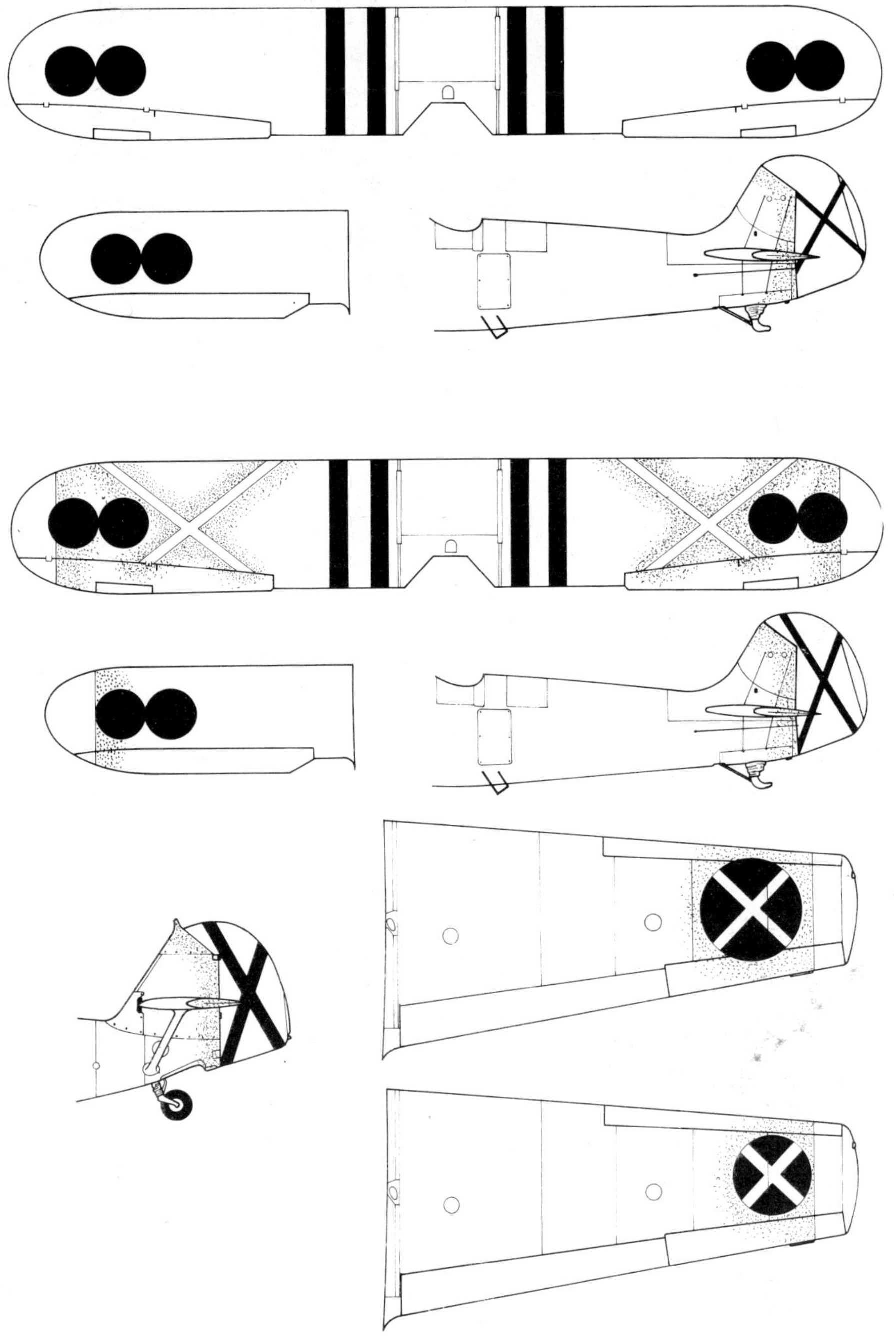

At the end of 1937 in Germany new type of camouflage was introduced, consisting of black-green (RLM 70) and dark green (RLM 71) on the upper surfaces and blue (RLM 65) on the undersides. A typical example was Messerschmitt Bf 109 B–2 of unteroffizier Erns Terry (6●38) fighting in 1. Squadron of J 88 (1./J 88).

There were probably a few Condor Legion Bf 109s painted in silver e.g. planes marked 6●6 and 6●12. Non-standard ways of painting we can met more often; probably Ar 68E 9●2 used in the Condor Legion as night fighter was overall in black; another untypical scheme was used on a He 45 C 15●10 of A/88 that was painted in irregular brown (RLM 61) areas, on the light grey (RLM 63) background, while a Heinkel He 51 2●59 was painted in RLM 62 Grün (or RLM 02 Grau) with brown areas on the upper wings and fuselage nose.

During the first period of fighting over Spain the predominant scheme on the bomber, attack and reconnaissance aircraft was in light grey-green (RLM 63) this including for example the Heinkel He 111, He 59 and He 46. This system was gradually replaced by a new scheme in which the upper surfaces and fuselage sides were painted in camouflage which consisted of scharp-edged areas in RLM 61/62/63, and undersides were finished in blue RLM 65, typical examples being the Junkers Ju 87, Dornier 17, Henschel 123, Ju 52 and Heinkel 111. Some other types, e.g. Fi 156 or Hs 126 of 1938 and 1939 were finished with

MARKINGS OF CONDOR LEGION AIRCRAFT

Bf 109B–2 of 2. Staffel J/88 Condor Legion, 1937. The aircraft was flown by Oblt. Walter Oesau. Camouflage typical for Messerschmitts in Condor Legion — light grey RLM 63. Note the non-standard cross of St. Andrew in the national marking on the wing undersurface. The fin bears 8 kill symbols.

(P. Jarrett via B. Ketley)

1234567890-

SHAPE OF NUMBERS USED IN FUSELAGE CODES OF *CONDOR LEGION* AIRCRAFT IN SPAIN, 1936–1939

1234567890

Light grey (RLM 63) Bf 109B–2 of 2./J 88 in flight over Spain during the Civil War. On the fuselage positioning and shape of the code number 6●52 is visible. The black marking on the fuselage has no white cross of St. Andrew, next to it the emblem of 2. Staffel – black tophat.

Below: Bf 109D of Condor Legion, again in light grey (RLM 63). *(both P. Jarrett via B. Ketley)*

their upper surfaces and sides in dark green (RLM 71), and undersides in blue (RLM 65).

All German aircraft of the Condor Legion were painted according to schemes used by the Luftwaffe, but were marked in the way specified for Franco's Air Forces, the insignia for which was a black St.Andrew's cross on the white background on the rudder. Supplementary identification markings were black discs painted on the upper and lower wings and the fuselage (sometimes the black circle contained the white St. Andrew's cross). Sometimes doubled circles of smaller diameter were applied. On some types (e.g. Heinkel 59, Heinkel 51) large white St. Andrew's crosses were painted on top of the wings directly on the camouflage background.

Attachment to a unit was signified by an emblem, e.g. the insignia of the 1st Squadron of 88 Fighter Wing (1./J 88) was a diving raven, 2./J 88 – a top hat, 3./J 88 – a Micky Mouse, and 4./J 88 – an ace of spades.

Other significant markings for Condor Legion aircraft were white wing tips and (sometimes) white spinners, treated as means of fast identification. Each aircraft belonging to the Legion had a type code number (e.g. the Messerschmitt Bf 109 was identified by black '6') painted near the black disc insignia on both sides of the fuselage. Codes used for identifying each type of aircraft used by the Condor Legion Condor are presented in the table; apart from the identity letter on the fuselage, individual number of the aircraft (e.g. 6●56) was also applied.

Emblem of 3. Staffel J/88 Condor Legion (Spain 1938) applied to fuselages of Messerschmitt Bf 109Ds and Cs, black 6 (the type code for 109 nationalist aviation) is visible. Next to the "Mickey Mouse" a word "Grazi" in small letters. *(P. Jarrett via B. Ketley)*